THE COLORFUL LOVE OF JESUS LIFTING UP WOMEN

The Connection of the Word with Colors

DOMINIQUE R. DELLA FERA

Books Academy LLC
112 SW H K Dodgen Loop,
Temple, Texas 76504
Hotline: (254) 800-1189

Ordering Information:
Quantity sales. Special discounts are available on quantity purchases by corporations, associations, and others. For details, contact the publisher at the address above.

Printed in the United States of America.

ISBN-13:	Softcover	978-1-964929-67-5
	eBook	978-1-964929-68-2

Library of Congress Control Number: 2024923242

A SPECIAL THANKS TO MY ABBA FATHER, MY PRECIOUS JESUS, AND MY SWEET PRECIOUS HOLY SPIRIT WHO WITHOUT THEM THIS BOOK WOULD HAVE NOT BEEN POSSIBLE. BLESSINGS! I LOVE YOU LORD AND I APPRECIATE ALL YOU HAVE DONE FOR ME, AND ALL THAT YOU ARE DOING AND ALL THAT YOU ARE GOING TO DO.AMEN AND AMEN!!!

A VERY SPECIAL THANKS AND A HEART FULL OF GRATITUDE TO MY BLESSED AND PRECIOUS SONS AUSTIN AND BROCK, WHO I LOVE WITH ALL MY HEART THEY HAVE NEVER GIVEN UP ON ME, JUST LIKE JESUS NEVER HAS, ALSO TO MY PRECIOUS GRANDCHILDREN FRANKIE AND LOUIE. NONA LOVES YOU VERY MUCH.

GOD'S BEST FOR YOU.

THIS BOOK IS ALSO IN LOVING MEMORY TO A PRECIOUS AND DEAR SISTER IN THE LORD, MISS SHIRLEY JOHNSON. SHE WAS A GREAT INSPIRATION FOR ME THROUGH THE HOLY SPIRIT TO WRITE THIS BOOK. I KNOW SHE IS LOOKING DOWN FROM THE GRANDSTANDS IN HEAVEN, JUST SMILING AND SAYING I KNEW YOU COULD DO IT. I JUST WANT TO SAY THANK YOU AND I APPRECIATE YOU.

LOVE YOU, SISTER DOMINIQUE

Contents

FORWORD

This book is dedicated to all the lonely, broken-hearted, abused women in this world, to let your Heavenly Father pour His Precious Love into you through His Only Begotten Son Jesus, and the anointing of the Sweet Precious Holy Spirit, who formed you, and knew you before the foundation of the world. He knew who your parents would be for He is the one who breathed life into you. Even if your earthly father rejected you, abandoned you, and if you have chosen men who did the same thing to you. Your Heavenly Father will never reject you. You are a special gift from the God of this whole Universe, who created it and everybody and everything in it. You are special like a precious gem in His sight. Doesn't matter where you have been, or what you have done, He is waiting for you to receive His love.

He loved you so much that He gave His only begotten Son Jesus, for you who went to the Cross and died and suffered what no man ever did or will again.

The Lord said no greater love then this then a man lay down His life for His friends and you are my friend. If you continue in me and I in you then you are my follower and you will know the Truth and Truth will set you Free.

Who I set Free is Free indeed. So if you were on the only woman in this world to receive His Great love He still would have done it for you. Praise the Name of Jesus!!!

He has a special purpose and plan for your life that only you can fulfill, and I declare and degree by faith that every woman that reads this book, will rise up and fulfill that call. You are beautifully and wonderfully made, you are His workmanship. He loves you with an everlasting love, He has your picture engrafted in the palm of His hand, and saved every tear you have ever shed in a bottle, and knows every hair on your head.

He said "Come unto me all who are heavy laden and I will give you rest for your souls (your mind, will and emotions) for my yoke is easy and my burden is light. Whatever you need come, and drink from the water I will give you and you will never thirst again come and dine with me Come to my banqueting table for you will never be hungry again for my banner over you is love, the love that this world cannot give to you. Everything He has made is beautiful and precious in His sight, for man looks at the outward appearance, but God looks at the heart.

He has called you out of the darkness of this world, out of all the troubles and fear and anxieties. Jesus always calls the hurting and the lonely and the rejected and what the world calls foolish.

For, He takes the foolish things to confound the wise. He usually takes the unqualified not all the time, but mostly because they are the ones who will receive His love. If you think you don't need Him and you can do this life on your own, then you won't call out to Him. He doesn't call perfect women, for many are called (which is the whole world) but few are chosen,(only the ones that will answer the call), then He will bring you into perfection in Him. Then in Him you will live and move and have your very being then He can show forth His Glory (which is all He has and all He is) in you to a lost and dying world. Accept His love today and accept Him not only as your Savior which He is, but as your Lord, King and Master and Everything, He is the potter and you are the clay, without Him you can do nothing, but with Him all things are possible

The colors God has created have meaning and through this book, you will see their meaning scripturally, and how under the presence of the Holy Spirit they will break bondages and destroy yokes, how Jesus has already set you free. So I speak healing to you Spiritually, Mentally and Physically, Abundant blessings in your life now and always, Jesus loves you and so do I. Your life will never be the same from this day forward I declare and degree it in Jesus Precious, Holy Name. Amen and Amen Love in Christ Dominique

INTRODUCTION TO COLORS

The reason I believe that the Lord led me to write this book on colors is, because they do have meaning and are more powerful then most of us have believed. We are surrounded by colors in this universe in our everyday lives, there are even more beautiful colors in Heaven then we can imagine right now. The Lord represents the Light of the world. He is surrounded by beautiful colors He gave us beautiful colors on this earth too, everything He created has beauty and a purpose for your life. This book will give you more understanding, revelation and depth on the colors. Why did he Lord used certain colors in the Old Testament in the Tabernacle, which is what we now call our Sanctuary today that is the Holy of Holies, we go in to meet with the presence of God. Why did the High Priests have to wear the prayer shawl of White and Blue and Gold, before they could enter into the Ark of the Covenant.

There was and is a special power and anointing of the Holy Spirit in those colors. God is a God of perfect order, and everything He does has order and in our lives, it should be the same because when there is lack of order, then confusion comes in and that is not of the Lord. He is not a confused God He knows everything from beginning to the end. Jesus is coming back for His Bride the Body of Christ, in White and Gold and riding a White horse, I believe that is His favorite color, just like the world's number one color is black and you will see what that means in the last chapter. The Churches will have an more understanding, they use certain colors for the Praise Dance and Flag Ministry, the Holy Spirit should direct them. They should pray before each service so they can be in one accord and unity. It is very important for everyone involved to put aside any differences, before they minister because of the effect you are making on people's lives. He knows the needs of the people in that particular service and what they are facing in their lives in that particular season.

Colors do help to break bondages and destroy yokes in your life, whatever you may be believing God for today there is a color you can wear. To put Him in remembrance of His word, which you always should be speaking His word over-your circumstances, but colors connect to His word, just for instance if a ministry sends you a prayer cloth for a certain need you are believing God for.

They are connecting their faith with yours and usually the prayer cloths are Red and White, you will see why after you finish reading this book. You can get in agreement with another sister to lay hands on you. With the color in a prayer cloth, or you can put that color on your body that relates to your need.

That just makes the anointing stronger on you, then believe God by faith to move in your situation. If you are led by the Holy Spirit wear that color that He directs you to. You can lay hands on yourself and speak the word over yourself and give birth to your miracle. I know Jesus is moving fast in these times because time is being compressed, even before you speak it and believe for whatever you may need it is coming to pass. You will look at the Blue and White sky in a new way and know that one of the meanings in the color Blue is for the Revealed will of God to be revealed on this earth

One of the meanings for the color White is light and why it covers the earth on a clear day when the sky is Blue and White why the grass is Green that is all around you, how in winter it loses its greenery and how in the Spring, it starts to become Green again because one of the things it means is New Beginnings. In that time of year after a long hard cold winter, people feel that everything starts coming back to life again. It is a time of Refreshing and Flourishing, which Green also relates to, you serve a very colorful and creative God. Everything He has done has a meaning He is truly a God of Perfect Order.

There is no confusion or shadow of turning in Him for what He has created. I am sure that the Garden of Eden, was full of colors and Green grass and trees, beautiful Blue and Green waters, beautiful flowers full of magnificent colors. Just like your heart is the Lord's Garden so if you plant good seed in good ground in your heart, you will have a beautiful garden growing constantly and such fabulous colors of flowers.

Pick out all of the weeds for they eat up your seed which is the word of God, you want that Garden of your Heart to remain beautiful for Him because that is what He always looks at the intentions of our hearts. So you don't want any evil thoughts to take root which is your weeds to choke out those beautiful flowers. For out of the abundance of the heart the mouth speaks. In this book I give you some scriptures that are associated with the colors, there are a lot more because I believe that colors are in direct connection with the word of God. They are like in one accord and you will understand that after you finish the book.

So I believe for God's revelation and knowledge to fill your heart to overflowing and before you select colors, around you for any purpose that the Holy Spirit will lead you to the colors, He wants you to surround yourself with. So don't let your world just be black and white add a lot of the right colors to it.

ABOUT THE AUTHOR

Dominique R. Della Fera has been serving the Lord since she received Jesus as her Lord and Savior in February in 1986. Before that she was raised in church but had stopped going, because she never knew Jesus as her Lord just as her Savior and really didn't know Him, and was really in rebellion, just doing what she wanted to do and living her life the way most people do, If they don't know Jesus. The Lord used someone who was very dear to her heart that He knew she would receive the truth from. For their life had turned around drastically, she wanted what they had to offer. So this person asked if they could come over the place where she was living with her two sons, Austin and Brockington.

So he proceeded to tell her about Jesus and His love for her in a way she had never heard it before. God knew how to reach her, but her two sons received Jesus first, that same afternoon right in their dining room. Austin was 14yrs. old and Brockington was 8 yrs old and also received the infilling in the baptism of the Holy Spirit speaking and praying in tongues. God has His own language just like He created all languages.

After the person left she accepted the Lord and two days later while running the vacuum cleaner in her dining room this unknown language just start flowing from her lips. Praise the Lord. She has been in her church for 16 yrs. She has been a greeter in the church, she has ushered when needed and done nursing home ministry, visitation and helped with baptisms' and also has been a Hostess for a few weddings. Also has done some decorating for Kenneth Hagin when he was alive preaching at her church.

She is also a graduate of World Harvest Bible Training Center. She is an evangelist and also has preached and sung praise and worship in the nursing homes and she does street ministry with her church and goes out and preaches the Gospel of Jesus Christ, which is good news. She has a ministry for hurting and abused woman called New Beginnings and Beauty for Ashes Ministries. Then when she was involved with the flag and praise dance ministry at her church, going to classes about the power and significance of the colors, God commissioned her to write this book. For all the women who are hurting and have been abused in His Kingdom and all over the world, His daughters are precious in His sight and He never intended for them to be abused. He loves His daughters with a most special and precious love.

AUTHOR'S TESTIMONY

I am writing some of my testimony in this book to give you insight into my life and what God has brought me through. In my darkest hour He has always been there for me and has given me His strength to make it. Just remember this, no matter who turns against you, whether it is a spouse or a child or a friend, Jesus will never turn against you. And if He is there for you, then who can be against you? "No one and nothing." Have faith and trust in Him and he will not and cannot forsake you. He will make a way of escape for you.

Some of you reading this book may have gone through more than I have and some less, but every one of us has dealt with rejection and painful life experiences. I will start with my childhood. I came from an Italian family in South Philadelphia. My grandparents came to America from Italy I was a little girl when they died. I never really knew them.

I lived in my grandparents' house. My grandmother had thirteen children. Six survived but seven didn't make it. Of those seven, my grandmother miscarried and the others were stillborn or lost to an illness shortly after being born. Of the 4 who returned to the house I was closest to my Aunt Grazia. She remained in the house and never married. My Mother raised me a good, little Catholic girl. I loved my mother but was close to my Aunt Grazia. She taught me to have faith and she always told me I could do it and I would make it. There were a lot of problems in the house and a lot of strife. Each of the siblings had their own lives and their own problems. Growing up I was very fearful, because of all the strife.

My father worked in New Jersey and my mother chose to stay in the house in South Philadelphia. My father loved me the best he knew how but he was divorced from my mother and had 5 other children that I rarely saw. But God restored that in my later years as I kept walking with Him. I have one brother I never met but I believe he is with Jesus now. My father lived in New Jersey and had a good job. He worked 10 days on and 3 days off, and that's when I'd see him. He was good to me in a lot of ways but he was a distant father.

Even so, I loved him.

In my heart I knew my father loved me and that I was very special to him. I was his precious daughter. But I think he was distant toward me, because of my upbringing. Remember, he was hardly ever there, and, in a way, when he was there, I was afraid of him. I wasn't quite thirteen when my father passed away on New Year's Day. I will never forget that day, I realize now it was after that, I began a spiral that was out of control.

I begin a series of relationships with men, looking for love in all the wrong places, and too many faces. The more I did that the worse it became. The more those rejection and lustful spirits came in, the more I realized I was looking for my father's love. Many men will tell you they love you if they think they can have sex with you. You may want the security of that feeling but it is fleeting. And afterward you feel even worse, if a man tosses you aside.

Your Heavenly Father is your answer. I believe the Lord protected me from so much, even when I was not serving Him, because until you know Him you will always see him as your earthly father. The Lord has protected me from 3 men who wanted to kill me. One was my neighbor who was abusing his wife and threatened to kill her and their children. I took the little girl to protect her, and the wife sought shelter by running into my house. The others were two men, were brothers who falsely accused me of doing something to their mother. That was not the facts. These things happened to me after I accepted Jesus, remember the devil is out to steal from you and the love that Jesus gave you so freely. The Word says that to whom much is given, much is required. The enemy was trying at that time to stop the call for my Ministry for Abused Women Even after you get saved, you may spirits in your life, from the past, (which are known as familiar spirits, that you will need to be delivered from, that only the Holy Spirit can show you what to do. God has always protected me from evildoers, and vindicated me. I thank Him because of the teaching I am under I know my authority in His word (which is Jesus) that they couldn't touch me.

There is a time to stay and stand and a time to shake the dust off your feet and let your peace return to you. Though many of these things were still happening in my life, it took me a while to walk in his Word. Even after I was saved, I was not set free instantly. The Devil will still try and put the same things in your path because he is not creative. If you do the same thing, you will achieve the same results. It is a daily walk to stay in the love of Jesus.

I was in an abusive marriage for over three years. Hardly any Christians understood, but the Lord released me from it. I suffered so much I thought I'd have to be put away. Praise the Lord I have the strength of Christ's power - love and a sound mind. So do you, but the word has to be worked and put into action and come out of your mouth. The Miracle is in your mouth.

My two sons, who did not live with me during those 3 years, saw the abuse and saw the pain I was in. I was forced out of the marriage and home. I was Blessed though, to go back in to the house where my sons lived with the man who raised them. The man who raised them is a man I was with for twenty years. He adopted my younger son and was with them through all the hard times. My children saw a lot of instability in my life and it affected them.

Now because of Jesus both are Blessed and Wonderful young men today. My younger son is a youth pastor and worship leader. He has written songs soon to be published and sang, for the Glory of God. My older son is a very smart businessman and is serving the Lord in leadership. Thank God for His Mercy, their life is much better than mine was, at their age.

Jesus has protected them, even when they were little from a lot of things, but he was not obligated to because I was not living for Him. As a child the Lord protected my life. I was almost run over by a car, the vehicle stopped right next to my body, which was flat on the ground next to the front tires, but I believe the ministering spirits stopped the car just in time. I did not have a scratch on my body.

Then there was a time I almost drowned but the waves carried me to my mother who was standing on the shore. There is just so much more of God's faithfulness and love because He knew one day I'd serve Him. Today my message to you is when people tell you that you are hopeless, God says you are not and it is never too late. I didn't get saved until I was 41 years old, around the same age as Moses when he came out of Egypt, so I am in good company.

When I did accept the Lord I saw a vision of a dozen red roses in a vision and a white dove, which represents, the Holy Spirit, He is the third person of the Godhead, that is one of the signs of His presence. Then the Red Roses which represents, Jesus and one of His names is the Rose of Sharon, because His blood has cleansed me from all unrighteousness.

When you come to Jesus that is just the beginning of your walk with Him. Salvation is a process, just like when Moses was in the desert and still in his soul area for another forty years, and then he walked in the spirit with the Lord for the last forty years. He was eighty when he began to walk in the spirit, listening and obeying God's voice.

I don't want that to be me but it has taken a while for me to walk in the deliverance of the Cross of Jesus. The more junk from the world there is, the harder it can be but, again, that is up to you. I was also into the witchcraft of reading cards but that is something that I learned from my family, but God delivered me from that not too long after I was saved.

Now He uses me to speak His word and to encourage and uplift other women in the prophetic anointing. God will use what satan has stolen from you and restore it and also use it for good to help other people. God is so wonderful.

His love is amazing. His loving kindness is better than life itself. We serve a God who is alive forevermore. He is always ready to heal and restore the broken dreams and pieces of your life.

He has healed my broken heart and He will do the same for you but you have to work with Him. The Word says Jesus came to heal the brokenhearted and set the captives free. I needed a lot of help so I was in my church as much as possible. Other things did not matter; I just wanted to know, more of the Word. I went to Bible School to get more revelation of the truth. I just can't get enough of Jesus and reading the word of God. Reading the Word every day and seeking the mind of Christ.

What would Jesus do in this situation? How did Jesus talk and walk? I pray for you that His light reveals the dark areas, in your heart that you become comfortable in, and used to doing and dispel evil patterns you have lived in for years. That have brought you sorrow and pain.

I pray in Jesus' name they are broken right now and you can name them and you are filled with the Holy Spirit to overflowing, and that you never get comfortable in your walk with Jesus but that you continually want to know His love. I declare it and I decree it and it shall be established in this life now.

Bless you. I hope and believe this has helped you to let you see you are not alone and that Jesus took all your pain and shame and refection at the cross, so give your guilt to Him. He will carry it for you so you won't have to, don't let the Devil lie to you anymore. Be free; be healed and delivered because you already are in Him. In Him you live and move and have your very being.

I love all of you, in Jesus love and believe for God's Almighty Power and Love to be strong in your lives. So, step up and out and over the bondage of rejection.

Blessings in the name of our Lord and Savior, Jesus Christ. Always remember He loves you.

1

GREEN

HEALING, NEW LIFE, NEW BEGINNINGS, PROSPERITY, HEALTH HOPE, RESTORATION, FLOURSHING, FRESHNESS, VIGOR, PRAISE, ETERNAL LIFE, MERCY, GOD'S HOLY SEED, HARVEST, SOWING AND REAPING .

Scriptures where the color Green is mentioned in the Bible:

Psalm 23:2 (KJV) He maketh me to lie down in Green pastures: He leadeth me beside the still waters.

Psalm 52:8 (KJV) But I am like A Green olive tree in the house of God: I trust in the mercy of God forever and ever.

Scriptures that pertain to the Color Green when you wear it:

HEALING

TOTAL HEALING FOR YOUR SPIRIT, SOUL (mind, will, and emotions) AND BODY.

Psalm 103:3 (KJV) Who forgives all thine iniquities; who Healeth all thy diseases.

Psalm 147:3 (KJV) He Healeth the broken in heart, and bindeth up their wounds.

Jeremiah 17:14 (KJV) Heal me, O Lord, and I shall be Healed; save me, and I shall be saved: for thou art my praise.

1 Peter 2:24 (KJV) Who His own self bare our sins in His own body on the tree that we, being dead to sins, should live unto righteousness: by whose stripes ye were Healed.

Psalm 107:19-20 (AMPLIFIED) Then they cry to the Lord in their trouble, and He delivers them out of their distresses. He sends forth His word and Heals them and rescues them from the pit and destruction.

Malachi 4:2 (AMPLIFIED) But unto you who revere and worshipfully fear My name shall the Sun of Righteousness arise with Healing in His wings and His beams, and you shall go forth and gambol like calves [released] from the stall and leap for joy.

Exodus 15:26 (KJV) And said, if thou wilt diligently hearken to the voice of the Lord thy God, and wilt do that which is right in His sight and wilt give ear to His commandments, and keep all His statutes, I will put none of these diseases upon thee, which I have brought upon the Egyptians; for I am the Lord that Healeth thee.

SUMMARY

Jesus took your Healing at Calvary, He bore your sicknesses and diseases, He took thirty-nine stripes on His back for the thirty-nine major diseases, that every other disease comes from (which is a spirit of infirmity) even the ones they have no name for. He carried them and took them for you, so that you don't have to, so when there is an attack against your physical body, (when you accepted Jesus) it is now a part of His body, because you are now a part of the Body of Christ and He is the Head.

He is the chief cornerstone, so your body is His temple, where He dwells and lives because it is in Him you live and move and have your being. You were bought and paid for with a heavy price because of His awesome love, so just thank Him for what He has already done for you, according to His word, It is a gift He gave to you even though you don't deserve it, so thank Him for those stripes, He took on His back, believe it and receive your Healing today in Jesus name. Blessings of that Healing walk in it. Amen

NEW LIFE

JESUS CAME TO GIVE YOU THAT NEW LIFE, A FRESH START IN YOUR LIFE, AND TO GIVE IT TO YOU MORE ABUNDANTLY.

Ezekiel 11:19 (AMPLIFIED) And I will give them one heart (a new heart) and I will put a new spirit within them; and I will take the stony (unnaturally hardened) heart out of their flesh, and will give them a heart of flesh (sensitive and responsive to the touch of their God).

Psalm 36:9 (KJV) For with thee is the fountain of life: in thy light shall we see light.

Ephesians 4:24 (KJV) And that ye put on the new man (or woman), which after God is created in righteousness and true holiness.

Psalm 91:16 (KJV) With long life will I satisfy him (or her) and show him (or her) my salvation.

Colossians 3:10(AMPL1FIED) And have clothed yourselves with the new (spiritual self), which is (ever in the process of being) renewed and remolded into (fuller and more perfect knowledge upon) knowledge after the image (the likeness) of Him Who created it.

Matthew 10:39 (AMPLIFIED) Whoever finds his (or her) (lower) life will lose it (the higher life); and whoever loses his (or her) (lower) life on my account will find it (higher life).

John 1:4-5 (KJV) In Him was life: and the life was the light of men (or women). And the light shineth in darkness; and the darkness comprehended it not.

John 8:12 (KJV) Then spake Jesus again unto them; saying I am the light of the world: he (or she) that followed me shall not walk in darkness, but shall have the light of life.

John 5:12 (KJV) He (or she) that hath the Son of Man hath life; and he (or she) that hath not the Son of God hath not life.

SUMMARY

Jesus came to give you New Life, so that your spirit would become alive unto Him. He set you free from the guilt and shame of your sinful nature and gave you His nature in you forevermore. Blessings, Blessings! Amen and Amen.

He came to proclaim liberty to the (physical and spiritual) captives. Setting the prisoners free and opening the eyes of the blind (physically and spiritually). Jesus took your Healing at Calvary. He gave you a New Life first Spiritually, Mentally and Physically. Salvation is for all the three parts of a man and woman. Blessings, Blessings!!!

NEW BEGINNINGS

GOD ALWAYS HAS NEW BEGINNINGS FOR YOU EVERY DAY, FOR HIS MERCIES ARE NEW EVERY MORNING.

Corinthians 5-17 (KJV) Therefore if any man is in Christ, he (or she) is a new creature: old things arc passed away; behold all things are become new.

Galatians 3-13 (AMPLIFIED) Christ purchased our freedom (redeeming us) from the curse (doom) of the law (and its condemnation) by (Himself) becoming a curse for us, for it is written (in the Scriptures). Cursed is everyone who hangs on a tree (is crucified).

Psalm 92 1-2 (KJV) It is a good thing to give thanks unto the Lord, and to sing praises unto thy name, O most High: To show forth thy loving-kindness in the morning and thy faithfulness every night.

Psalm 96 1-2 (KJV) O Sing unto the Lord a new song: sing unto the Lord, all the earth. Sing unto the Lord, Bless His Name; show forth His Salvation from day to day.

Psalm 95 1-2 (KJV) O Come, let us sing unto the Lord: let us make a joyful noise to the rock of our salvation. Let us come before His Presence with thanksgiving, and make a joyful noise unto Him with palms.

SUMMARY

With the Lord, no matter what you have done, even if you knew Him before and turned your back on Him. He is always waiting for you to return to Him. There is always a New Beginning with God. He will never turn you away. If you come to Him with a repentant heart and ask His forgiveness, then you will be back in right standing with the Father because of Jesus, accepting His Love for you, and He is the God of New Beginnings.

Knowing that you serve a forgiving God who loved you more then His life and suffered the shame and pain for you, so, remembering that there is nothing too hard for Him. Blessings, Blessings! Amen and Amen.

PROSPERITY

JESUS SAID AS YOUR SOUL PROSPERS, SO WILL YOU PROSPER AND HAVE GOOD SUCCESS, IN THIS LIFE HERE AND NOW AS YOU RENEW YOUR MIND TO THE WORD OF GOD.

Isaiah 26:3 (KJV) Thou wilt keep him (or her) in perfect peace whose mind is stayed on thee; because he (or she) trusteth in thee.

Deuteronomy 29:9 (AMPLIFIED) Therefore keep the words of this covenant and do them that you may del wisely and Prosper in all that you do.

Joshua 1:7-8 (KJV) Only be thou strong and very courageous, that thou mayest observe to do according to all the law, which Moses my servant commanded thee: turn not from it to the right hand or to the left, that thou mayest Prosper whithersoever thou goest. This book of the law shall not depart out of they mouth: but thou shalt meditate therein day and night, that thou mayest observe to do according to all that is written therein: for then thou shalt make thy way Prosperous, and then thou shalt have good success.

Psalm 1:3 (KJV) And he (or she) shall be like a tree planted by the rivers of water, that bringeth forth his (or her) fruit in his (or her) season; his (or her) leaf also shall not wither; and whatsoever he (or she) doeth shall Prosper.

Psalm 122:6-7 (AMPLIFIED) Pray for the peace of Jerusalem! May they prosper who love you [the Holy City]! May peace be within your walls and Prosperity within your palaces!

Job 36:11 (AMPLIFIED) If they obey and serve Him, they shall spend their days in Prosperity and their years in Pleasantness and Joy.

SUMMARY

It is the Lord's will for you to have Prosperity and He said but first seek the Kingdom of God and His Righteousness, and all these things shall be added unto you. He also said I will never see the righteous forsaken or begging for bread. So He wants to Bless you Abundantly with All Spiritual Blessings, as it is in Heaven so shall it be done on earth and Heaven is rich beyond compare, but so is this vast universe that God has created for you, but seek spiritual prosperity first, seek the Lord with all your heart, soul and strength, and prosperity is not just concerning earthy things It is also peace for your mind in the middle of the storms in life, and the trials. That's when the Lord said my peace passes all human understanding and His joy is your strength.

For this is the season and the time for the wealth of the sinner that is laid up for the just, whatever seed you or your ancestors have sown for the Gospel's sake will be multiplied back to you for this is harvest time. For the plowman is overtaking the reaper, whatever seed that has been sown is coming back to you, more then you could ask or think, saith the Lord. This is the seventh last great wealth transfer to God's people, for those who are obedient to His voice and to sow what the Lord tells you to for the Kingdom of God, according to the Power that worketh in you.

So expect it and receive it in Jesus Name. Blessings overtake you and your family that you don't have room enough to receive or contain them.

Overflowing so you can be a Blessing to other people. Amen and Amen.

HEALTH

JESUS TOOK YOUR HEALING, SO YOU COULD WALK IN DIVINE HEALTH.

Proverbs 12:18 (KJV) There is that speaketh like the piercings of a sword: but the tongue of the wise is Health.

Jeremiah 30:17 (KJV) For I will restore Health unto thee, and I will Heal thee of thy wounds, saith the Lord; because they called thee an Outcast, saying. This is Zion, whom no man seeketh after.

James 5:16 (KJV) Confess your faults one to another, and pray one for another, that ye may be Healed. The effectual fervent prayer of a righteous man (or woman) availeth much.

SUMMARY

Jesus took all your diseases (which is a lack of ease in your body and mind) at Calvary. He already bore it for you, so don't have to bare that spirit of infirmity. Don't deny the facts but you choose, its your choice to believe the truth. So receive that Blessings of Divine Health today and walk in it in Jesus Name. Blessings, Blessings! Amen and Amen.

HOPE

FAITH MOTIVATES YOUR HOPE, WITHOUT FAITH YOU WILL NOT HAVE HOPE, AND CANNOT PLEASE GOD.

Psalm 33:22 (KJV) Let thy mercy, O Lord, be upon us, according as we hope in thee.

Psalm 31:24 (KJV) Be of good courage, and He shall strengthen your heart, all ye that Hope in the Lord.

Psalm 42:5 (AMPLIFIED) Why are you cast down, O my inner self? And why should you moan over me and be disquieted within me? Hope in God and wait expectantly for Him, for I shall yet praise Him, my Help and my God.

Psalm 43:5 (KJV) Why art thou cast down, O soul? And why art thou disquieted within me? Hope thou in God: for I shall yet praise Him, who is the health of my countenance, and my God.

SUMMARY

In every situation in this life we have to have Hope, because if we become hopeless we just don't want to go on anymore. That is why I believe people self-destruct in their lives. Our Hope is in God the maker of Heaven and Earth When we put our Hope and Faith and Trust in Him, we will be confident that He will work all things out to good to those who love the Lord and are called to His Purpose and His Plan for their lives. Amen and Amen

RESTORATION

THE LORD WILL RESTORE EVERYTHING, THAT THE DEVIL HAS STOLEN FROM YOU. JUST CONTINUE IN HIM BECAUSE IT'S IN HIM WE LIVE AND MOVE AND HAVE OUR BEING.

1John 10:10 (AMPLIFIED) The thief comes only in order to steal and kill and destroy. I came that they may have and enjoy life, and have it in abundance (to the full, till it overflows).

Proverbs 6:31 (KJV) But if he be found, he shall Restore sevenfold; he shall give all the substance of his house.

Psalms 23:3 (AMPLIFIED) He refreshes and Restores my life (my self); He leads me in the paths of righteousness [uprightness and right standing with Him not for my earning it, but] for His name's sake.

Deuteronomy 28:2-9 (KJV) And all these Blessings shall come on thee, and overtake thee, if thou shalt hearken unto the voice of the Lord thy God.

Blessed shalt thou be in the city, and Blessed shalt thou be in the field. Blessed shall be the fruit of thy body, and the fruit of thy ground, and the fruit of thy cattle, the increase of thy kind, and the flocks of thy sheep.

Blessed shall be thy basket and thy store. Blessed shall thou be when thou comest in, and Blessed shalt thou be when thou goest out. The Lord shall cause thine enemies that rise up against thee to be smitten before thy face: they shall come out against thee one way, and flee before thee seven ways.

The Lord shall command the Blessing upon thee in thy storehouses and in all that thou stets thine hand unto; and He shall Bless thee in the land which the Lord thy God giveth thee. The Lord shall establish thee a holy people unto Himself, as He hath sworn unto thee, if thou shalt keep the commandments of the Lord thy God, and walk in His ways.

SUMMARY

The Lord wants to Restore all the broken pieces of your life, and your dreams that the enemy (the devil) has stolen, because he is the thief and he only comes to kill, steal and destroy. Jesus came to Restore everything back to mankind and womankind to give back everything Adam forfeited to the devil. He has taken it back and Restored what the enemy has stolen from you.

So walk in His ways, and His ways are much higher then your ways. Hear the voice of the Good Shepherd, and the voice of the stranger you will not follow. So hearken diligently to His voice, listen to the Sweet Precious Holy Spirit for He is a perfect gentleman. He will never push you to do something or make a decision. He will gently lead you with peace, the peace that passes all your natural understanding, in the midst of the storm. I speak complete Restoration in your life for what you are believing Jesus for in His holy precious name.

Blessings, Blessings! Amen and Amen.

FLOURSHING

THE LORD WANTS YOU TO FLOURISH AND PROSPER, IN EVERYTHING YOU PUT YOUR HANDS TO AND EVERYWHERE, THE SOLES OF YOUR FEET WALK ON.

Psalms 92:14-15 (KJV) They shall still bring forth fruit in old age: they shall be fat and flourishing. To show that the Lord is upright: He is my rock, and there is no unrighteousness in Him.

Psalms 92:14-15 (AMPLIFIED) [Growing in grace] that they shall still bring forth fruit in old age: they shall be full of sap [of spiritual vitality] and [rich in the] verdure [of trust, love, and contentment]. [They are living memorials] to show that the Lord is upright and faithful to His promises: He is my Rock, and there is no unrighteousness, In Him.

SUMMARY

The Lord said you will Flourish in all things and bare much fruit for His kingdom especially in your older age. Because by that time you have learned how to trust Him more, seeing that He hasn't failed you and cannot fail you if you believe His word. You have experienced more of His awesome love. His faithfulness in all things in your life, it is also never too late to start serving Jesus with all your heart. He will bless the fruit of your hands, and your children and your family and to a thousand generations, if He tarries.

In these last days of the world the way you knew it, He is Blessing His people abundantly. So it might as well be you, so Blessings falling and coming to you like showers of rain, of His mercy, grace and truth. Blessings, Blessings! Amen and Amen.

FRESHNESS

JESUS WANTS YOU TO BE REFRESHED BY THE WORD OF GOD, WHICH IS THE LIVING WATER THE WASHING OF THE WATER OF THE WORD.

Psalm 36:9 (KJV) For with thee is the fountain of life: in thy light shall we see light.

Proverbs 13:14 (KJV) The law of the wise is a fountain of life, to depart from the snares of death.

Jeremiah 2:13 (KJV) For my people have committed two evils; they have forsaken me the fountain of living waters, and hewed them out cisterns, broken cisterns, that can hold no water.

Revelation 21:6 (KJV) And he said unto me; It is done, I am Alpha and Omega, the beginning and the end. I will give unto him that is athirst of the fountain of the water of life freely.

SUMMARY

Jesus is the word made flesh. He brings life to you and health to all your flesh. His word brings refreshing to your spirit, soul and body. Fresh anointing will come through the Sweet Precious Holy Spirit.

Refresh yourself anew today and everyday with the giver of life for He will bring freshness to the broken dreams of your life. You can dream again, all things are possible if you believe. Be refreshed Blessings overtake you Amen and Amen.

VIGOR

JESUS WILL GIVE YOU DIVINE ENERGY AND STRENGTH, WHEN YOU ARE WEARY, YOU ARE ONLY STRONG IN THE LORD, AND THE POWER OF HIS MIGHT.

Ephesians 3:16 (AMPLIFIED) May He grant you out of the rich treasury of His Glory to be strengthened and reinforced with mighty power in the inner man by the (Holy) Spirit (Himself indwelling your innermost being and personality).

Psalm 18:32 (KJV) It is God that girdeth me with strength, and maketh my way perfect.

Psalm 27:1 (KJV) The Lord is my Light and my Salvation; whom shall I fear? The Lord is the Strength of my life; of whom shall I be afraid?

Psalm 28:7 (AMPLIFIED) The Lord is my Strength an my (impenetrable) Shield; my heart trusts in, relies on, and confidently leans on Him, and I am, helped; therefore my heart greatly rejoices, and with my song will I praise Him.

Psalm 46:1 (KJV) God is our refuge and strength, a very present help in trouble.

Revelation 4:12 (KJV) Saying with a loud voice, Worthy is the Lamb that was slain to receive power, and riches and wisdom and strength, and honor, and glory, and blessing.

Isaiah 35:3-4 (KJV) Strengthen ye the weak hands, and confirm the feeble knees. Say to them that are of a fearful heart. Be strong, fear not: behold, your God will come with vengeance, even God with recompense; He will come and save you.

SUMMARY

Jesus tells us when you are weak lean on His Strength for He will renew your youth with the strength of an eagle. He renews our vigor and vitality when we allow God's Spirit to keep you strong. When the Spirit is willing but the flesh is weak, then you know that Jesus is inside of you and has carried you through. Be strong in the Lord and the power of His Might always. May the King of Kings and Lord of Lords bless you withHis love.

PRAISE

THE LORD INHABITS THE PRAISE OF HIS PEOPLE. HE ACTUALLY DWELLS IN YOUR PRAISE, THE PRAISE GOES UP AND THE BLESSINGS COME DOWN.

Psalm 111:1 (KJV) Praise ye the Lord, I will praise the Lord with my whole heart, in the assembly of the upright, and in the congregation.

Psalm 112:1 (KJV) Praise ye the Lord, Blessed is the man (or woman) that feareth the Lord that delighteth greatly in His commandments.

Psalm 113:1 (KJV) Praise ye the Lord, Praise, O ye servants of the Lord, praise the name of the Lord. Blessed be the name of the Lord from this time forth and for evermore. From the rising of the sun unto the going down of the same the Lord's name is to be praised.

Psalm 117:1-2 (KJV) O Praise the Lord, all ye nations praise Him, all ye people. For His merciful kindness is great toward us: and the truth of the Lord endureth forever. Praise ye the Lord.

SUMMARY

When the devil throws all of his firery darts keep praising the Lord, and you will see your circumstances change. That is why the Bible says offer a sacrifice of Praise, when your heart is breaking, and you are weary and you feel like giving up, and the enemy is telling you that you are a failure. And what God told you won't work to just forget it and let it go Keep Praising Him don't stop and do it with the joy of the Lord and you will see the shackles of the enemy fall. When the Praise goes up the blessings of God come down. So matter what happens,

Praise Jesus and He will bless you and never fail you. Praise is your weapon against the evil one. The Israelites walked around the walls of Jericho seven times and just kept Praising God. With a shout of triumph out loud and didn't stop till the walls came down and the walls in your life will come down too. Bless You. Amen and Amen!!!

ETERNAL LIFE

THE LIFE OF JESUS IS WITHIN YOU WHICH IS EVERLASTING LIFE, ETERNAL LIFE, IN THE SPIRIT YOU ARE SEATED IN HEAVENLY PLACES, RIGHT NOW WITH HIM IF HE LIVES AND DWELLS WITHIN YOUR HEART.

John 6:40 (KJV) And this is the will of Him that sent me, that every one which seeth the Son, and believeth on Him may have everlasting life: and I will raise Him up at the last day.

1 Peter 5:10 (KJV) But the God of all grace, who hath called us unto His Eternal Glory by Christ Jesus, after that ye have suffered a while, make you perfect, establish, strengthen, and settle you.

1 John 1:2 (AMPLIFIED) And the Life ("an aspect of His being) was revealed (made manifest, demonstrated), and we saw (as eyewitnesses) and are testifying to and declare to you the Life, the Eternal Life (" in Him). Who already existed with the Father and Who (actually) was made visible (was revealed) to us (His followers).

1 John 5:11 (KJV) And this is the record, that God hath given to us Eternal Life, and this life is in His Son.

SUMMARY

Jesus came to not only give you Eternal Life, not only when you go to Heaven, but Eternal Life is in you now. His Resurrection Power that raised Jesus from the dead lives in you. If you have accepted the great sacrifice when Jesus shed His Blood at the Cross. He is the Lamb of God that was slain for you and for me. He was innocent without sin He knew no sin but became sin for you so, you can have everlasting life with Him forever and ever. Amen

MERCY
THE LORD'S MERCY ENDURES FOREVER, FOR HIS LOVING KINDNESS IS BETTER THEEN LIFE BECAUSE WITHOUT IT THEY WOULD BE NO LIFE.

Psalm 118:1 (KJV) O Give thanks unto the Lord, for He is good: because His Mercy endureth forever.

Psalm 138:8 (KJV) The Lord will perfect that which concerneth me: Thy Mercy, O Lord endureth forever: forsake not the works of Thine own hands.

Psalm 145:8-9 (KJV) The Lord is gracious, and full of compassion: slow to anger, and of great Mercy. The Lord is good to all: and His tender Mercies are over all His works.

SUMMARY

Jesus Mercy is over the whole world and His Mercies are new every morning to you. If you do something wrong His Mercy and Grace (God's unmerited favor even though we didn't deserve it) is always there for you. So keep running to His Mercy Seat in the time of need, For His Mercy hovers over you.

Hosanna in the Highest! His loving kindness which is His Mercy is better then life itself Without His Mercy on you and me everyday starting before, He formed you and knew you, and knew all about your life form beginning to the end. He still loved you much more then you loved yourself. What an Awesome Father and Big Brother, Jesus and the Wonderful Sweet Holy Spirit, who is always waiting for you to call on Him in time of trouble.

Blessings, Blessings! Amen and Amen

GODS HOLY SEED

JESUS IS THE WAY, THE TRUTH AND THE LIFE AND NO MAN (OR WOMAN), COMES TO THE FATHER BUT THROUGH THE SON.

Matthew 1:21 (KJV And she shall bring forth a Son, and thou shalt call His Name Jesus for He shall save His people from their sins.

Corinthians 12:3 (KJV) Wherefore I give you to understand, that no man speaking by the Spirit of God calleth Jesus accursed: and that no man can say that Jesus is the Lord, by the Holy Ghost.

Hebrews 12:2 (AMPLIFIED) Looking away (from all that will distract) to Jesus. Who is the Leader and the Source of our Faith (giving the first incentive for our belief) and is also its Finisher (bringing it to maturity and perfection).He, for the joy (of obtaining the prize) that was set before Him, endured the Cross, despising and ignoring the shame. And is now seated at the right hand of the throne of God.

SUMMARY

Jesus is Father God's, First Holy Seed but when you accept Jesus Love for you. Jesus becomes not only your Lord and Savior, but also your Big Brother. Now the Lord says be ye Holy unto me, even as I am Holy which is your reasonable service.

The Lord doesn't see you anymore as a dirty rotten sinner, but He sees you as His Saint. Saved by His Grace, He sees the whole world as His Saints. He died for everyone but it is up to them to accept His Great Love.

That is why He is believing at the final judgment not to say depart from me I never knew you. You don't have to be that person, just accept Jesus in your heart today and your life will never be the same. Hosanna to His Highest the King of Kings and the Lord of Lords.

Blessings, Blessings! Amen and Amen.

HARVEST

JESUS WAS AND IS THE HOLY SEED OF FATHER, GOD GIVEN FOR THE WORLD WHICH IS THE HARVEST OF SOULS.

Genesis 8:22 (KJV) While the earth remaineth, seedtime and harvest, and cold and heat, and summer and winter, and day and night shall not cease.

Matthew 9:37-38 (KJV) Then He saith unto His disciples. The Harvest truly is plenteous, but the laborers are few; Pray ye therefore the Lord of the Harvest, that He will send forth laborers into His Harvest.

Revelation 14:15 (KJV) And another angel came out of the temple, crying with a loud voice to Him that sat on the cloud. Thrust in thy sickle, and reap: for the time is come for thee to reap; for the Harvest of the earth is ripe.

SUMMARY

Jesus said this is the end time harvest to reach out to this lost and dying world. You are one of the laborers in His vineyard. So this is seedtime and harvest. This is the season and the time for Jesus Great Love to flow through you to reach all the people around you. In your walk everyday with Him, and the prophets of old were waiting to see what you are seeing today.

All the Signs, Wonders and Miracles, You will continue to see more of God's Glory then ever before all the souls coming into the Kingdom. This is the best time to be alive for a believer, for the Prophets of old will say these are the ones that seen the Glory fall. Blessings, Blessings! Amen and Amen.

SOWING AND REAPING

THE WORD SAYS WHATEVER YOU SOW YOU WILL REAP, WHATEVER SEEDS YOU ARE PLANTING IN YOUR LIFE. YOU WILL SEE THEM COME BACK TO YOU, RIGHT OR WRONG, GOOD OR BAD, THAT IS WHY YOU ALWAYS WANT TO SOW GOOD FRUIT IN THE LIVES OF OTHERS, SO YOU CAN HAVE A GOOD HARVEST IN YOUR LIFE HERE AND NOW.

Psalm 126:5 (AMPLIFIED) They who sow in tears shall reap in joy and singing.

Corinthians 9:6 (AMPLIFIED) (Remember) this: he who sows sparingly and grudgingly will also reap sparingly and grudgingly, and he who sows generously (that blessings may come to someone) will also reap generously and with blessings.

Galatians 6:7 (AMPLIFIED) Do not be deceived and deluded and misled; God will not allow Himself to be sneered at (scorned, disdained, or mocked by mere pretensions or professions or by His precepts being set aside.) He inevitably deludes himself (herself) who attempts to delude God.) For whatever a man (or woman) sows, that and that only is what he (or she) will reap.

James 3:18 (AMPLIFIED) And the harvest of righteousness (of conformity to God's will in thought and deed) is (the fruit of the seed) sown in peace by those who work for and make peace (in themselves and in others, that peace which means concord, agreement, and harmony between individuals, with undisturbedness, in a peaceful mind free from fears and agitating passions and moral conflict.

Hosea10:12(AMPLIFIED) Sow for yourselves according to righteousness (uprightness and right standing with God): reap according to mercy and loving-kindness. Break up your uncultivated ground, for it is time to seek the Lord, to inquire for and of Him, and to require His favor till He comes and teaches you righteousness and rains His righteous gift of salvation upon you.

John 4:36-37 (KJV) And he that reapeth receiveth wages, and gathereth fruit unto life eternal: that both he that soweth and he that reapeth may rejoice together, And herein that saying is true. One soweth, and another reapeth.

Galatians 6:7-10 (KJV) Be not deceived; God is not mocked: for whatsoever a man soweth, that shall he (or she) also reap. For he(or she) that soweth to his(or her) flesh shall of the flesh reap corruption; but he(or she) that soweth to the Spirit shall of the Spirit reap life everlasting. And let us not be weary in well doing: for in due season we shall reap, if we faint not. As we therefore have opportunity, let us do good unto all men, especially unto them that are of the household of faith.

SUMMARY

Jesus has told us that there is seedtime and harvest, sowing and reaping and that is in everything we do not just with your money, but with your time and talent and how you respond to people everyday. Your attitude determines your altitude. Jesus said to make peace with all men and women if possible.

Display Jesus love, kindness, His mercy and His grace because He loves you no matter what you do or have done or will ever do. He is always there with His arms open wide to you. He will never leave you or forsake you even if you don't feel His Presence sometimes start praising Him and you will get into His presence. In His Presence is fullness of Joy. Blessings, Blessings!!!

Amen and Amen.

EPILOGUE ON THE COLOR GREEN:

The color Green is a Healing color and gives you a New Hope again which renews your Faith in the Lord. Without Faith we cannot please Him and you love Him because He first loved you. There is nothing you did or ever could do to repay Him. When you see the Spring of the Year coming in and all the Green Trees and Grass that is a New Beginning in the earth and also Restoration and Healing.

I believe that is why the Lord made the Trees and Grass Green to give the earth a New Hope every year. It is also around the time of the Jewish Passover which has many Blessings connected to it. That is why believe

He said in Psalm Twenty Three, I will make you lie down in Green Pastures, Pastures of Refreshing that are Flourishing. Hosanna to the Highest Blessings, Blessings, and Abundant Blessings like Showers of Rain on you and your family Amen and Amen.

2

RED

BLOOD OF JESUS, ATONEMENT, POWER, WARFARE, COMSUMING FIRE, PASSION, THE CROSS OF JESUS, LOVE, AND MARTYRED SAINTS.

Scriptures where the color Red is mentioned:

Exodus 26:14 (KJV) And thou shalt make a covering for the tent of rams" skin dyed red, and a covering above of badger's skin.

Numbers 19:2 (KJV) This is the ordinance of the law which the Lord hath commanded, saying, Speak unto the children of Israel that they bring thee a red heifer without spot, wherein no blemish is, and upon which never came a yoke.

Scriptures that pertain to the color Red when you wear it:

BLOOD OF JESUS

THE POWER THAT IS IN THE BLOOD, THAT WAS SHED SEVEN TIMES, AND EACH TIME GOD HAS SET YOU FREE FROM ALL BONDAGES.

Hebrews 9:12-14 (AMPLIFIED) He went once for all into the (Holy of) Holies (of heaven), not by virtue of the blood of goats and calves (by which to make reconciliation between God and man), but His own blood, having found and secured a complete redemption (an everlasting release for us). For if (the mere) sprinkling of unholy and defiled persons with blood of goats and bulls and with the ashes of a brunt heifer is sufficient for the purification of the body. How much more surely shall the Blood of Christ, Who by virtue of (His) eternal Spirit (His own preexistent divine personality) has offered Himself as an unblemished sacrifice to God, purify our consciences from dead works and lifeless observances to serve the (ever) living God?

Leviticus 17:11 (KJV) For the life of the flesh is in the blood: and I have given it you upon the altar to make an atonement for your souls: for it is the blood that maketh an atonement for the soul.

Revelation 1:5-6 (KJV) And from Jesus Christ, who is the faithful witness, and the first Begotten of the dead, and the prince of Kings of the earth. Unto Him that loved us, and washed us from our sins in His own Blood. And hath made us Kings and Priests unto God and His Father; to Him be Glory and Dominion for ever and ever. Amen

SUMMARY

The Blood of Jesus has cleansed us from all unrighteousness He has washed us clean and pure in His sight. He doesn't see our sins anymore once you have surrendered your life for His. So be free in Him, cleansed and pure in His sight now and forever more. And it will never lose its power it reaches to the highest mountains in your life and to the lowest valleys. Blessings! Blessings! Amen and Amen.

ATONEMENT

JESUS ULTIMATE SACRIFICE FOR YOU ON THE CROSS.

Leviticus 16:11 (KJV) And Aaron shall bring the bullock of the sin offering, which is for himself, and shall make an Atonement for himself and for his house, and shall kill the bullock of the sin offering which is for himself.

Numbers 8:19 (AMPLIFIED) And I have given the Levites as a gift to Aaron and to his sons from among the Israelites, to do the service of the Israelites at the Tent of Meeting and to make Atonement for them, that there may be no plague among the Israelites if they should come near the sanctuary.

Hebrews 9:12-14 (KJV) Neither by the blood of goats and calves, but by His own Blood He entered in once into the holy place, having obtained eternal redemption for us For if the blood of bulls and of goats, and the ashes of an heifer sprinkling the unclean, sanctifieth to the purifying of the flesh: How much more shall the Blood of Christ, who through the Eternal Spirit offered Himself without spot to God, purge your conscience from dead works to serve the living God, purge your conscience from dead works to serve the living God?

Hebrews 9:22 (AMPLIFIED) (In fact) under the Law almost everything is purified by means of blood, and without the shedding of blood there is neither release form sin and its guilt nor the remission of the due and merited punishment for sins.

SUMMARY

Jesus was and is the final Atonement, for your sins past, present and future every precious drop of His Blood that was shed for all mankind and womankind. Because of His Blood we are made whiter than snow cleansed from all unrighteousness.

Now we can come boldly into the throne room, in the time of need. He ever liveth, to make intercession for His Saints and He says to Father God not guilty. Blessings, Blessings!!!Amen and Amen.

POWER

JESUS IS THE LIGHT OF THE WORLD. HE IS LIKE A BEACON, IN HIS NAME LIES ALL THE SPIRITUAL POWER, YOU WILL EVER NEED IN THIS LIFE.

Psalm 62:11 (KJV) God hath spoken once; twice have I heard this; that power belongeth unto God.

Romans 1:16 (KJV) For I am not ashamed of the gospel of Christ: for it is the power of God unto salvation to every one that believeth; to the Jew first, and also to the Greek.

Ephesians 1:19 (KJV) And what is the exceeding greatness of His power to us-ward who believe, according to the working of His Mighty Power.

Philippians 3:10 (AMPLIFIED) (For my determined purpose is) that I may know Him (that I may progressively become more deeply and intimately acquainted with Him, perceiving and recognizing and understanding the wonders of His Person more strongly and more clearly), and that I may in that same way come to know the Power Overflowing from His Resurrection (which it exerts over believers), and that I may so share His sufferings as to be continually transformed (in spirit into His likeness even) to His death (in the hope).

2 Timothy 1:7 (AMPLIFIED) For God did not give us a spirit of timidity (of cowardice, of craven and cringing and fawning fear), but (He has given us a spirit) of power and of love and of calm and well-balanced mind and discipline and self-control.

Jude 1:25 (AMPLIFIED) To the only God, our Savior through Jesus Christ our Lord, be Glory (splendor), majesty, might and dominion, and power and authority, before all time and now and forever (unto all the ages of eternity). Amen (so be it).

SUMMARY

All power in Heaven and Earth belongs to your Lord and Savior Jesus Christ and through Him we have that same (Dunamis) Power because greater is He that is in you then he that is in the world. Through Him all things are possible, that same Power that raised Christ from the dead is in you.

Jesus said let your Light shine that you may be known of all men and women, don't hide under a bushel but let the world see that Jesus is Alive and Well and sits on the right hand of Father God Forever and Ever Amen and Amen

WARFARE

JESUS ALREADY DEFEATED SATAN, SO YOU FIGHT THE GOOD FIGHT OF FAITH. THE BATTLE IS THE LORD'S JUST KEEP HIS PRAISE ONS YOUR LIPS, AND HIS WORD ON YOUR LIPS AND IN YOUR HEART

Galatians 2:20 (AMPLIFIED) I have been crucified with Christ (in Him I have shared His Crucifixion): it is no longer I who live, but Christ (the Messiah) who lives in me; and the life I now live in the body I live by faith in (by adherence to and reliance on and complete trust in) the Son of God, Who loved me and gave Himself up for me.

Galatians 3:11 (AMPLIFIED) Now it is evident that no person is justified (declared righteous and brought into right standing with God) through the Law, for the Scripture says, The man (or woman) in right standing with God (the just, the righteous) shall live by and out of faith and he (or she) who through and by faith is declared righteous and in right standing with God shall live.

Ephesians 6:16 (KJV) Above all, taking the Shield of Faith, where with ye shall be able to quench all the fiery darts of the wicked.

2 Corinthians 5:7 (AMPLIFIED) For we walk by faith (we regulate our lives and conduct ourselves by our conviction or belief respecting man's (or woman's) relationship to God and Divine things, with trust and Holy Fervor, thus we walk) not by sight or appearance.

2 Corinthians 10:3 -5 (KJV) For though we walk in the flesh, we do not war after the flesh. (For the weapons of our warfare arc not carnal, but mighty through God to the pulling down of strongholds;) Casting down imaginations, and every high thing that exalt itself against the knowledge of God, and bringing into captivity every thought to the obedience of Christ.

SUMMARY

Jesus has already defeated Satan. He died and was buried and went into hell and took the Keys of sin, the grave and death from the devil so you cannot fight an enemy that has already been defeated. Remember, the battlefield is in the mind you have to cast down every thought, that is against the word of God. The devil is a deceiver and whatever he tells you it is the opposite of what God says in His Word.The devil wants you to get your eyes on .his lies. You fight the good fight of faith reminding him that Jesus stripped him at the Cross, and his future is hell and that yours is as bright as the promises of the Most High God, the living God. For if it isn't written it isn't real. When Jesus was in the wilderness for forty days and forty nights, He said to Satan it is written man (or woman) does not live by bread alone but by every word that proceeds out of the mouth of God. The weapon against Satan is the word of God; it pierces through any darkness in your life. Use and believe it, not sometime but all the time and you will be victorious in Christ. I believe your word is true in Jesus Name. Blessings, Blessings!

CONSUMING FIRE

GOD WILL STOP YOUR ENEMIES FROM DOING YOU ANY HARM.

Exodus 3:2-3 (KJV) And the angel of the Lord appeared unto him in a flame of fire out of the midst of a bush: and he looked, and behold, the bush burned with fire, and the bush was not consumed.

Acts 2:2-4 (KJV) And suddenly there came a sound from Heaven as of a rushing mighty wind, and it filled the entire house where they were sitting. And there appeared unto them cloven tongues like as of fire, and it sat upon each of them. And they were all filled with the Holy Ghost, and began to speak with other tongues, as the Spirit gave them utterance.

SUMMARY

Your God is a consuming fire, and He surrounds you with His Ministering Spirits (angels) as you speak the Word of God. The angels go to work for you getting rid of the things that try to stop your walk, with the Lord. He surrounds you with the Fire of the Holy Ghost. The devil can't stop you, the Lord watches over you and keeps you under the shadow of His Wings. Now and Always. Be Blessed Amen and Amen

PASSION

JESUS HAD COMPASSION FOR EVERYONE, THAT WAS BROUGHT TO HIM, FOR HE IS DIVINE LOVE IN ACTION.

Luke 18:38-43 (KJV) And he cried, saying, Jesus, thou son of David, have mercy on me. And they which went before rebuked him, that he should hold his peace: but he cried so much the more, Thou son of David, have mercy on me. And Jesus stood, and commanded him to be brought unto him: and when he was come near, he asked him, Saying, What wilt thou that I shall do unto thee? And he said, Lord, that I may receive my sight. And Jesus said unto him, receive thy sight: thy faith hath saved thee. And immediately he received his sight, and followed him, glorifying God: and all the people, when they saw it, gave praise unto-God.

SUMMARY

Divine Compassion and a Passion for people, which is Divine Love in action. He went about doing good healing all that were oppressed of the Devil for God was with Him. That is what He is Divine Love that is His Personality. Bless you. Amen and Amen.

THE CROSS OF JESUS

WHAT JESUS DID FOR YOU ON THE CROSS HOW HE SET YOU FREE, FROM ALL UNRIGHTEOUSNESS.

Isaiah 54:3-5 (AMPLIFIED) He was despised and rejected and forsaken by men a Man of sorrows and pains, and acquainted with grief and sickness: and like One from whom men hide their faces He was despised, and we did not appreciate His worth or have any esteem for Him. Surely He has borne our (grief's weaknesses, and distresses) and carried our sorrows, and pains (of punishment), yet we (ignorantly) considered Him stricken, smitten, and afflicted by God (as if with leprosy).

But He was wounded for our transgressions, lie was bruised for our guilt and iniquities; the chastisement (needful to obtain) peace and well-being for us was upon Him, and with the stripes (that wounded) Him we are Healed and Made Whole.

SUMMARY

Jesus took it all for you, so that in every situation you have the victory. You are not trying to get it. He already has done it. He says Stand Still and see the Salvation of your Lord and Savior, Jesus Christ that every knee shall bow and every tongue confess that He is the Lord of All.

LOVE

THE GREAT LOVE OF JESUS IS UNCONDITIONAL NOT BECAUSE OF ANYTHING YOU HAVE DONE, BUT BECAUSE WHAT HE HAS DONE FOR YOU. HE FIRST LOVED YOU WITH AND EVERLASTING LOVE.

Ephesians 3:17-20 (AMPLIFIED) May Christ through your faith (actually) dwell (settle down, abide, make His permanent home) in your hearts! May you be rooted deep in lover and founded securely on love. That you may have the power and be strong to apprehend and grasp with all the saints (God's devoted people, the experience of that love) what is the breadth and length and height and depth (of it);

That you may really come to know (practically, through experience for yourselves) the love of Christ, which far surpasses (mere knowledge, without experience); that you may be filled (through your being) unto all the fullness of God (may have the richest measure of the Divine Presence, and become a body wholly filled and flooded with God Himself)!

Now to Him Who, by (in consequence of) the (action of His) power that is at work within us, is able to (carry out His purpose and) do superabundantly, far over and above all that we (dare) ask or think (infinitely beyond our highest prayers, desires, thoughts, hopes, or dreams).

SUMMARY

Jesus says to you, you are my friend, and whatever you need me to be. When you are sad, I will dry your tears. When you are scared I will comfort your fears. When you are worried, I will give you hope. When you are confused, I will help you cope. For when you feel that you are lost. and can't see the light. I shall be you beacon. Blessings to you falling on you and overtaking you like showers of rain. Amen and Amen.

MARTYRED SAINTS

ALL THE CHRISTIANS THAT WERE MARTYRED FOR THEIR FAITH IN THE OLD AND NEW TESTAMENTS, AND EVEN TODAY BEING PERSECUTED FOR THEIR BELIEF IN JESUS.

Revelation 17:6 (KJV) And I also saw the woman drunken with the blood of the Saints and with the blood of the Martyr's of Jesus: and when I saw her, I wondered with great admiration.

Psalm 97:10 (KJV) Ye love the Lord, hate evil: He preserveth the souls of His Saints; He delivered them out of the hand of the wicked.

1 Corinthians 6:2 (AMPLIFIED) Do you not know that the Saints (the believers) will (one day) judge and govern the world? And if the world (itself) is to be judged and ruled by you, are you unworthy and incompetent to try (such petty matters) of the smallest courts of justice?

Revelation 19:7-8 (AMPLIFIED) Let us rejoice and shout for joy (exulting and triumphant)! Let us celebrate and ascribe to Him Glory and Honor, for the marriage of the Lamb (at last) has come, and His bride has prepared herself. She has been permitted to dress in fine (radiant) linen, dazzling and white for the fine linen is (signifies, represents) the righteousness (the upright, just, and godly living, deeds, and conduct, and right standing with God) of the Saints.

SUMMARY

Remember all the Precious Saints that gave their lives for the sake of the Gospel of Christ. When you are being persecuted for the word of God count it all Joy, knowing this that the word of God will never return void. It is light and it always overcomes the darkness in this world. We do suffer persecution for the word's sake just like the religious leaders in Jesus time when they said about Him.

Who does he think he is? Well, Jesus knew who He was. When you are walking in the fullness of the Gospel people will say the same about you. When you know who you are in Christ it doesn't matter what people think about you just pray for them. For they know not what they do, the Lord said touch not mine anointed and do my Prophets no harm. He means exactly what He said and also when you pray for them, you keep bitterness out of your own heart. Jesus said Bless your enemies, Bless and curse not, Love your enemies you may not like them, but Love them anyway in the Love of Jesus that has been shed abroad in your heart by the Holy Ghost. Bless You Amen and Amen.

EPILOGUE FOR THE COLOR RED:

In this chapter you have seen the power in the color Red. I believe that because of the meanings of Red it has boldness. Red represents the Blood of Jesus, which represent His Great Love for you and His Passion on the Cross. Also they use that color on Valentine's Day for sweethearts because of it representing Love and Passion for each other. It is a strong color also reminding you of the Saints that gave their lives for the Gospel because they would not deny the power of their Risen Lord and Savior and that your God is a consuming fire.

If you let Him, He will remove and burn out all the dross in your life to make you a vessel of pure gold, shiny and new without any flaws or imperfections. Wear Red boldly, it is a cleansing color always making you brand new again constantly renewing you and changing you into His image and after His likeness.

Be that shiny light in the dark places of this world. I believe that Red is one of God's favorite colors, it reminds Him of His Love and Passion for you and what He has done for you after all He is the lover of your soul. He is the author of romance and no romance novel can compare to His love for you, so ask Him to wrap His loving arms around you today. He will and He will tell you how much, because His love never ends, always was and always will be.

He loves you but be sure to tell Him how much you love Him. Tell Him everyday how much you love Him and how grateful you are for His Great Compassion (Divine Love in Action). Bless the Lord always, and tell Him how much you appreciate Him, You are only here for His Glory and to enjoy what He has created for you, and He has done what no other person can or will ever do for you.

FINAL EPILOGUE FOR THE COLORS RED AND GREEN: WHICH ARE ASSOCIATED WITH THE CHRISTMAS COLORS. THAT ARE USED EVERY YEAR .

Well, in reading the last two chapters of this Book, I know you will understand why they are used for celebrating Jesus birth. When He came into this world for you and for me. Now when we look at the color Red, most people associate it with Love and of course Jesus loved you enough to come down in human form into this world. Where He knew He was just passing through to do the will of the Father who sent Him and also for the Great Love He shed at the Cross. No Greater Love was ever displayed in the History of this world, or will ever be again.

He was the ultimate sacrifice of man and womankind. Red also represents the Cross of Jesus Christ and every drop of blood shed for you, me, and the whole world. His passion for you to suffer the shame and pain to set you free, He paid the price to cleanse you from all unrighteous, and all stain of sin. He is the atonement. He is the Consuming Fire which Red also means.

So at Christmas time when you celebrate with Red that should remind you of the Precious Blood of the Lamb of God. His Great Passion for you. I believe that most women when they love a man and get married to him they want to feel and know, that the man would lay down his life for her, if he had to, but Jesus is the one who already did that for both of you. Jesus made the Love between a man and woman to be beautiful and romantic. Enjoy each other and be secure in that love.

Be free to love each other. He laid His life down for both of you. He didn't have to but He still did, He is the ultimate lover of your soul and is everything you need Him to be and He wants you to be content in Him. By putting Him first in your life and for Him to fill you to overflowing with His love, Be content in Him first in your life and let Him fill you to overflowing in His love first, not to be looking to another person for that I am not saying as Christians that we shouldn't love on each other because Jesus said we should.

If you are looking to get married, you and that other person should compliment each other together in the Holy Spirit. Know what your vision is and if His compliments with yours for the Glory of God. Love one another in His love putting the other person ahead of your self. Not in the ways of the fleshly kind of desires to put your self first, but in the spiritual desires.

Jesus put you before Himself and wants you to do the same thing that is why the Lord says offer your bodies as a living sacrifice. If you notice around Christmas time people are more considerate of other people they are not as rude, are more courteous towards others give of themselves more. Put all kinds of bright lights on their houses and are all around more friendly.

Jesus is the Light of this dark world and people feel that and celebrate that, but if Jesus is in your heart, then Christmas is every day and you will always be looking for ways to Bless someone, with His Love and show kindness,

His Love is the greatest gift of all. Have a very Blessed and Prosperous Christmas everyday of the year. Bless You. Spread His Love and let this be the best Christmas of your life. Let it be a New Beginning for you and your family. From now on believe that each Year will be better and better for the rest of your life or until Jesus comes, that is the Lord's will for you. He said in Jeremiah, I have come to give you a future and a hope and a expected end that all your dreams and visions will be fulfilled in this life as well as in eternity. So wear your Red this year with Holy Boldness, knowing that if you believe in Him, that His love has been shed abroad in your Heart forever. Blessings! Blessings!

Now the color Green, which also is associated with the Christmas season, because when Jesus was born in the Little Town of Bethlehem almost 2,000 years ago. He gave new hope to the world. He represented the symbol of Healing, Restoration, New Beginning and a New Life for all of us. He is God's Holy Seed. These are some of the meanings the rest you have just read. He is the Healer for this world. He came to bring healing, which is His Love into men and women's hearts.. But only you can receive His Love and accept it, no-one else can do it for you.

Jesus came to give you Eternal Life restoring you to the Father, in Holiness and Oneness and Completion. He wants you to have that Eternal Life, that comes within you when Jesus comes and resides in your heart, which is Righteousness, Peace and Joy in the Holy Ghost

That is the Kingdom of God in Heaven, also at Christmas time people put holly out or a holly wreath, which is usually Green and then there is the mistletoe, which is Red and Green. When you put that out it is hanging up so, if you pass under it with someone they have to give you a kiss, as an expression of Love. Green is also Sowing and Reaping, God gave His only Begotten Son as a seed on this earth He sowed the best Seed He had, which is Jesus to Reap the whole world to Himself . But still some people have not received this Love. They are looking for other things to fill their empty hearts.

When the Greatest Seed was already Sown to Reap the Harvest of Souls for His Kingdom. He doesn't want any to perish but sadly they are perishing everyday, because of lack of Revelation and Knowledge. That is even why God's people in the Body of Christ are destroyed for lack of Knowledge in the Wisdom of God. In the Book of Proverbs, the Lord tells you that Wisdom is the Principle thing above all else. You need God's Wisdom in this life in everything you do. That only comes through the Anointing of the Sweet Precious Holy Spirit, when you ask Him to guard your heart, for out of it flow the issues of life. So you want Him to direct and guide your paths in the right direction that you need to take in every area. When you put your Christmas tree up this year, and if you use

Green and Red lights on your Green Tree, you will know more of the meaning of the tree and the lights. Green also means Praise that is why you sing Christmas Spiritual Songs to Praise the Lord for His birth and

Sowing His Precious Son. That is also why I like to look at the Color Green to receive His Love and know that the Precious Baby Jesus was Down for me. If I would have been the only person to receive Him, He still would have come into this world for me.

So receive this Precious Baby this year as the Seed Sown for you. Thanking Him for doing what He did, make it personal make this Christmas a Joyous and Blessed Season, not just because of the presents under the tree. But for the best present you could ever receive, from now on and everyday. He loves you and I can't say that enough.

For you are Precious in His sight, now and always. Be thankful always have an attitude of gratitude in your life for all He has done and will do for you.

For He will never leave you or forsake you, even if your family has, or if they have abused you as a child. His arms are open wide to you now and always, even if you walk away from Him, He will always try to woo you back. I love you in His love and Jesus definitely loves you the most Blessings of Peace, Love and Joy to you forever in this life and certainly in the next!

3

PURPLE

ROYALTY, KINGSHIP, MAJESTY, WEALTH, KINGLINESS, POWER, MEDIATOR, PENITENCE, THE NAME OF GOD, KINGDOM AUTHORITY, DOMINION, SONSHIP, THE PROMISES OF GOD, AND INTERITANCE.

Scriptures where the color Purple is mentioned in the Bible:

Exodus 28:8 (KJV) And the "curious girdle of the epod, which is upon it, shall be of the same, according to the work thereof, even of gold, of blue, and purple, and scarlet, and fine twined linen.

Esther 8:15 (KJV) And Mordecai went out from the presence of the king in royal apparel of / blue and white, and with a great crown of gold, and with a garment of fine linen and Purple, and the city of Shushan rejoiced and was glad.

Mark 15:17 (AMPLIFIED) And they dressed Him in (a) Purple (robe) and, weaving together a crown of thorns, they placed it on Him. And they began to salute Him, Hail (greetings. Good Health to You, Long Life to You), King of the Jews.

Scriptures that pertain to the color Purple when you wear it:

ROYALTY

JESUS WAS CLOTHED IN PURPLE, BECAUSE HE IS THE KING OF KINGS AND THE LORD OF LORDS.

Revelation 1:8 (KJV) I am Alpha and Omega, the beginning and the ending, saith the Lord, which is, and which was, and which is to come, the Almighty.

Revelation 1:5-6 (KJV) And from Jesus Christ, who is the faithful witness, and the First Begotten of the dead, and the Prince of the Kings of the earth. Unto Him that loved us, washed us from our sins in His own Blood. And hath made us Kings and Priests unto God and His Father; to Him be Glory and Dominion forever and ever. Amen.

1 Peter 2:9 (KJV) But ye are a chosen generation, a Royal Priesthood, an Holy Nation, a Peculiar people; that ye should show forth the praises of Him who hath called you out of darkness into His marvelous light:

Acts 2:8 (KJV) If ye fulfill the royal law according to the scripture, Thou shalt love thy neighbor as thyself, and ye do well

SUMMARY

Jesus is the King of Kings and Lord of Lords, He made you Holy unto Himself. He made you His royalty. You are His ambassador for His Kingdom, the Kingdom of Heaven. You are a peculiar people (which means possessed by Him). He said go into all the nations of the earth and preach this Gospel of the Kingdom. When you stand before the Kings and Queens, I will give you the words to speak and I will fill your mouth. He has set us on High with Him. May the Blessings of His Royalty abound in your life. Amen and Amen

KINGSHIP

JESUS IS THE KING OF KINGS AND THE LORD OF LORD'S, IF YOU ARE IN HIS KINGDOM, THEN YOUR ARE MADE IN HIS IMAGE AND AFTER HIS LIKNESS

Revelation 1:6 (AMPLIFIED) And formed us into a Kingdom (a royal race), priests to His God and Father—to Him be the Glory and the Power and the Majesty and the Dominion throughout the ages and forever and ever. Amen (so be it).

Revelation 1:8 (AMPLIFIED) I AM THE Alpha and the Omega, the Beginning and the End, says the Lord God. He who is and who was and who is to come, the Almighty (the Ruler of all).

1 Peter 2: 9 (AMPLIFIED) But you are a chosen race, a royal priesthood, a dedicated nation, (God's) own purchased, special people, that you may set forth the wonderful deeds and display the virtues and perfections of Him who called you out of darkness into His marvelous light.

Exodus 19: 5-6 (AMPLIFIED) Now therefore, if ye will obey My voice in truth and keep My covenant, then you shall be My own Peculiar Possession and Treasure form among and above all peoples; for all the earth is Mine. And you shall be to Me a Kingdom of Priests, a Holy Nation (consecrated; set apart to the worship of God). These are the words you shall speak to the Israelites.

SUMMARY

Jesus said you are a King (or Queen) unto Him. We rule and reign with Him right now in His Kingdom so you are royalty, because He is above every King (or Queen) in this world and the next.

You are to proclaim His authority in this earth, everywhere you go because even though you are in your earthly body, you are still seated in Heavenly Places with Him. He said greater works will you do then I did, because I go to My Father and Your Father. May His Blessings overtake you .Hosanna, Hosanna, Amen and Amen.

MAJESTY

EXALT LIFT UP ON HIGH THE NAME OF JESUS, THE KINGDOM AUTHORITY, JESUS WHO DIED NOW GLORIFIED.

Psalm 21:5-6 (AMPLIFIED) His Glory is great because of your aid; Splendor a Majesty You bestow upon Him. For you make Him to be blessed and a Blessing forever; you make Him exceedingly glad with the joy of Your Presence.

Psalm 93:1 (KJV) The Lord reigneth, He is clothed with Majesty; the Lord is clothed with strength, wherewith He hath girded Himself: the world also is established, that it cannot be moved.

Psalm 145:12 (KJV) To make known to the sons of men His Mighty Acts, and the Glorious Majesty of His Kingdom.

SUMMARY

Jesus is clothed in a Robe of Righteousness and He gave you that Beautiful Robe of Righteousness that His Glory, which is the Glory of the Father, be revealed. This means all God has and all that He is, His Majesty shown in and through you. Blessings, Blessings! Amen and Amen.

WEALTH

JESUS TOOK OUR POVERTY, AT THE CROSS WITH THE CROWN OF THORNS, AND HE HAS GIVEN US THE POWER TO CREATE WEALTH AND THE ABILITY, FOR YOU TO WALK IN ABUNDANCE. BUT FIRST AND FOREMOST TO BE A BIG GIVER TO HIS KINGDOM, TO ESTABLISH HIS COVENANT ON THIS EARTH.

Deuteronomy 9:18 (KJV) But thou shalt remember the Lord thy God: for it is He that giveth thee the power to get wealth that He may establish His covenant which He sware unto thy fathers, as it is this day.

Deuteronomy 8:7-10 (KJV) For the Lord thy God bringeth thee into a good land, a land of brooks of water, of fountains and depths that spring out of valleys and hills. A land of wheat, and barley, and vines, and fig trees, and pomegranates: a land of oil olive, and honey. A land wherein thou where thou shalt eat bread without scarceness, thou shalt nor lack anything in it; a land whose stones are iron, and out of whose hills thou mayest dig brass. When thou hast eaten and art full, then thou shalt Bless the Lord thy God for the good land which He hath given thee.

Deuteronomy 8:17 (AMPLIFIED) And beware lest you say in your (mind and) heart. My power and the might of my hand have gotten me this Wealth.

1 Corinthians 10:24 (AMPLIFIED) Let no one then seek his (or her) own good and advantage and profit, but (rather) each one of the other (let him (or her) seek the welfare of his (or her) neighbor.

SUMMARY

The Lord wants you to have more then enough. He wants His Blessings to overtake you. He has given you the Power and Ability to create Wealth to establish His Kingdom. He never intended for the Body of Christ to be on barely getting along street. He wants you to rule and reign on this earth as Priest's and King's (or Queen) so that the world can see you serve the King of Kings, and the Lord of Lords, but you have to expect that from the Lord and believe His Word.

Be obedient on your giving your tithes and offerings, and there is nothing that you need that He doesn't already have, and if He doesn't have it, He will create it for you. He will give you a creative idea and witty invention. Your cup should be running over, constantly overflowing of Blessings, so you can be a Blessing to someone else. Blessings overflow in your life. Amen and Amen

KINGLINESS

JESUS SHOWED YOU HOW TO BE THE KIND OF LEADER THAT HE DEMONSTRATED. HE WAS A SERVANT, AND THAT IS WHAT A GOD LEADER IS THAT IS WHY HE SAID I CAME NOT TO BE SERVED, BUT TO SERVE THAT HIS LIFE WOULD BE A RANSOM FOR MANY TO SERVE AND TO SHOW HIS LOVE .

Isaiah 32:1 (KJV) Behold, a King shall reign in righteousness and princes shall rule in judgment.

Isaiah 33:22 (KJV) For the Lord is our judge, the Lord is our lawgiver, the Lord is our King; He will save us.

1 Timothy 6:11-12 (KJV) But thou, O man (or woman) of God, flee these things: and follow after Righteousness, Godliness, Faith, Love, Patience, and Meekness. Fight the Good Fight of Faith, lay hold on Eternal Life, whereunto thou art also called, and hast professed a good profession before many witnesses.

SUMMARY

Jesus said to be a Leader you must first be a Servant in His Kingdom to many. He also said before Honor comes Humility, which means to be Humble, to be Teachable in the Things of God, to respect the Authority over you and to be Submissive. He will promote you in due season. He is a God of Perfect Order. Blessings, Blessings! Amen and Amen.

POWER

THE POWER OF THE BELIEVER IS IN THE NAME OF JESUS, AND THROUGH HIS BLOOD, WITH THE WORD OF YOUR TESTIMONY. (WHICH IS WHAT JESUS HAS DONE IN YOUR LIFE), AND THAT HE HAS ALREADY SET YOU FREE FROM SIN AND SPIRITUALLY DEATH.

Mark 16:17-18 (KJV) And these signs shall follow them that believe. In my Name shall they cast out devils, they shall speak with new tongues. They shall take up serpents and if they drink any deadly thing it shall not harm them, they shall lay hands on the sick, and they shall recover.

Isaiah 40:29-31 (KJV) He giveth power to the faint; and to them that have no might He increaseth strength.

Even the youths shall faint and be weary, and the young men shall utterly fall: But they that wait upon the Lord shall renew their strength: they shall mount up with wings as eagles; they shall run, and not be weary; and they shall walk, and not faint.

Matthew 28:1 8-20 (KJV) And Jesus came and spake unto them, saying, all power is given unto Me in Heaven and in Earth. Go ye therefore, and teach all nations, baptizing them in the name of the Father, and of the Son, and of the Holy Ghost. Teaching them to observe all things whatsoever I have commanded you: and, lo, I am with you always, even unto the end of the world, Amen

John 1:12 (AMPLIFIED) But to as many as did receive and welcome Him, He gave the authority (power, privilege, right) to become the children of God, that is, to those who believe in (adhere to, trust in, and rely on) His Name.

SUMMARY

You have power in the Name of Jesus to put the devil on the run and under your feet. Jesus said all power in Heaven and Earth has been given to me and I give it to you. Sometimes you may put up with things you don't have to, because Jesus already took it for you.

He stripped Satan of his power and knocked out all his teeth, he can only gum you, the word says he comes in as a roaring lion but he is not a roaring lion. Jesus is the Lion of the tribe of Juda. He already won the battle so the battle is the Lord's not yours. So trust in Him today whatever you are facing knowing, He has already defeated Satan. You cannot lose when you use His Name and His Blood.

Take your rightful authority because it belongs to you. Bless you Jesus loves you and so do I. Amen and Amen. .

MEDIATOR

THERE IS ONY ONE MEDIATOR BETWEEN GOD AND MAN, (OR WOMAN) YOUR LORD AND SAVIOR JESUS CHRIST AND HE IS RISEN AND ALIVE FOREVERMORE.

Timothy 2:5 (KJV) For there is one God, and one Mediator between Christ-Jesus.

Hebrews 9:15 (AMPLIFIED) (Christ the Messiah) is therefore the Negotiator and Mediator of an (entirely) new agreement (testament, covenant); so that those who are called and offered it may receive the fulfillment of the promised everlasting inheritance— since a death has taken place which rescues and delivers and redeems them from the transgressions committed under the (old) first agreement.

Hebrews 12:24 (KJV) And to Jesus the Mediator of the New Covenant, and to the blood of sprinkling that seeketh better things than that of Abel.

SUMMARY

Jesus is on the throne He is your Mediator before the Father day and night. He doesn't sleep or slumber. He ever liveth to plead your cause. Call on His Precious Name today and He will and cannot fail you, because He is the Way, the Truth and the Light, He cannot lie. He will do what He said He will do in His Word, because He is the Word made flesh, so call on Him today. Blessings, Blessings! Amen and Amen.

PENITENCE

GOD AND HIS SAINTS JUDGING THE WORLD, AND WHOEVER DID NOT RECEIVE, HIM WILL HAVE REPENTANCE FOR ALL ETERNITY.

Matthew 9:11-13 (AMPLIFIED) And when the Pharisees saw this, they said to His disciples. Why does your Master eat with tax collectors and those (preeminently) sinful? But when Jesus heard it, He replied, those who are strong and well (healthy) have no need of a physician, but those who are weak and sick. Go and learn what this means; I desire mercy (that is, readiness to help those in trouble) and not sacrifice and sacrificial victims.

For I came not to call and invite (to repentance) the righteous (those who are upright and in right standing with God), but sinners (the erring ones and all those not free from sin).

Hosea 6:6 (AMPLIFIED) For I desire and delight in dutiful steadfast love and goodness, not sacrifice, and the knowledge of and acquaintance with God more than burnt offerings.

Acts 11:18 (KJV) When they heard these things, they held their peace, and glorified God, saying, then hath God also to the Gentiles granted repentance unto life.

Peter 3:9 (KJV) The Lord is not slack concerning His Promise, as some men count slackness; but is longsuffering to us-ward, not willing that any should perish, but that all should come to repentance.

SUMMARY

There is coming a time when Jesus will judge the whole world with His Saints. That will be the time of penitence for whoever did not accept His love at the Cross. Even though it is not His Will for anyone to perish, but to have everlasting life. He does not violate your will to accept His Love or His Blood that was given and shed for you, so you could come to repentance. For He took your penitence so that you didn't have to, He is the Living Atonement that took your place and mine. Blessings of His Love overtake you always.

THE NAME OF GOD

THE LORD HAS MANY NAMES BECAUSE IN HIS NAMES, IS EVERYTHING WE NEED HIM TO BE.

Psalms 8:1 (AMPLIFIED) O Lord, our Lord, how excellent (majestic and glorious) is Your Name in all the earth! You have set Your Glory on (or above) the Heavens.

Psalm 72:17 (KJV) His Name shall endure for ever: His Name shall be continued as long as the sun; and men shall be blessed in Him: all nations shall call I him blessed.

Psalm 106:8 (KJV) Nevertheless He Saved them for His Name's sake, that He Might make His Mighty Power to be known.

Psalm 132:2 (KJV) I will worship toward thy Holy Temple, and Praise thy Name for thy Loving-kindness and for thy Truth: for thou hast Magnified thy Word above all thy Name.

Proverbs 22:1 (KJV) A Good Name is rather to be chosen than great riches, and loving favor rather than silver and gold.

Isaiah 9:6 (KJV) For unto us a child is born, unto us a son is given; and the government shall be upon His shoulder: and His Name shall be called Wonderful, Counselor, The Mighty God, The Everlasting Father, and The Prince of Peace.

John 20:31 (KJV) But these are written, that ye might believe that Jesus is the Christ, the Son of God; and that believing ye might have life through His Name.

Philippians 2:9-11 (KJV) Wherefore God also hath highly exalted Him, and given Him a Name which is above every Name: That at the Name of Jesus every knee should bow, of things in Heaven, and things in earth, and things under the earth: And that every tongue should confess that Jesus Christ is Lord, to the Glory of God the Father.

SUMMARY

In the Precious Name of Jesus you have everything you need, Jesus said if you have seen me you have seen the Father and if you will hear my voice, you hear the Father and everything I do is what my Father tells me to do. The Lord has many names in the Old Testament. A few of His names are Jehovah, Yahweh, Yeshua, Elohim (Almighty God), Adonai, and El Shaddai (which is the all sufficient One); these are just a few. He said to Moses when He asked Him His Name, He said, "I am that I am". He is everything to you in everything you need Him to be in every situation of your life. There are all kinds of Blessings in His Name. Amen

KINGDOM AUTHORITY

JESUS SAID AS IT IS IN HEAVEN SO SHALL IT BE DONE IN EARTH.

Matthew 16:19 (AMPLIFIED) I will give you the keys of the Kingdom of Heaven; and whatever you bind (declare to be improper and unlawful) or (declare lawful) on earth must be what is already loosed in Heaven.

Romans 14:17 (KJV) For the Kingdom of God is not meat and drink: but righteousness, and peace, and joy in the Holy Ghost.

Colossians 1:10-13 (KJV) That ye might walk worthy of the Lord unto all pleasing, being fruitful in every good work, and increasing in the knowledge of God: Strengthened with all might, according to His Glorious Power, unto all patience and longsuffering with joyfulness: Giving thanks unto the Father, which hath made us meet to be partakers of the Inheritance of the Saints in Light. Who hath delivered us from the power of darkness, and hath translated us into the Kingdom of His Dear Son.

SUMMARY

Jesus gave us His Kingdom Authority to rule and reign in this earth over all the power of the enemy the devil. He said that as believers when we speak the word of God the angels will start to work for you. He gave us the Keys to His Kingdom and the Kingdom of God is within you when you have Jesus. Hosanna, Hosanna, Amen and Amen.

DOMINION

YOU HAVE POWER AND AUTHORITY IN THE NAME OF JESUS.

Ephesians 6:10 (KJV) Finally my brethren, be strong in the Lord, and in the power of His Might.

JESUS IS SPEAKING TO YOU

Mark 11:23-26 (KJV) For verily, I say unto you. That whosoever shall say unto this mountain. Be thou removed, and be thou cast into the sea, and shall not doubt in his (or her heart but shall believe that those things which he saith shall come to pass, he (or she) shall have whatsoever he (or she) saith.

Therefore I say unto you. What things so ever ye desire, when ye pray, believe that ye receive them, and ye shall have them. And when ye stand praying, forgive, if ye have aught against any: that your Father also which is in Heaven may forgive you your trespasses. But if ye do not forgive, neither will your Father which is in Heaven forgive your trespasses.

SUMMARY

The Lord is saying we have power in the name of Jesus to turn circumstances around and things that the devil does to try and hinder or stop our living for Jesus or causes division in the Body of Christ or in our or to put distractions to abort your faith on the dreams and visions that God has promised you, His purpose and plan for your life.

He cannot stop you if you stand rooted and grounded in Christ who is the word made flesh. Jesus said you must also forgive anyone who has wronged you according to the word of God. Also He wants you not retain that sin against them, that is not based on feelings it is in faith asking God to give you His forgiveness in your heart for that person.

That is not an option but a commandment to go to that brother or sister and try to make it right if they reject you then you still have done the right thing before God and then that is between them and God. Pray for them that will keep bitterness from staying in your heart. Blessings, Blessings! Amen, an Amen.

SONSHIP

ALMIGHTY GOD IS YOUR FATHER AND JESUS IS YOUR BIG BROTHER.

Matthew 18:19-20 (KJV) Verily I say unto you. Whatsoever ye shall bind on earth shall be bound in Heaven: and whatsoever ye shall loose on earth shall be loosed in Heaven. Again I say unto you. That if two of you shall agree on earth as touching any thing that they shall ask, it shall be done for them of my Father which is in Heaven. For where two or three are gathered together in my name, there am I in the midst of them.

Proverbs 4:10 (KJV) Hear, O my son (or daughter) and receive my saying; and the years of thy life shall be many.

Proverbs 4:20-22 (KJV) My son or daughter attend to my words: incline thine ear unto my sayings. Let them not depart from thine eyes, keep them in the midst of thine heart for they are life unto those that find them, and health to all their flesh.

JESUS IS SPEAKING TO YOU

John 10:9-11 (KJV) I am the door: by me if any man enter in, he (or she) shall be saved, and shall go in and out, and find pasture. The thief cometh not, but for to steal, and to kill, and to destroy; I am come that they might have life, and that they might have it more abundantly. I am the Good Shepherd: the Good Shepherd giveth His life for the sheep.

SUMMARY

Father God is our Father when we accept Jesus in our hearts and His great Love. Go to your Father today and if you ask Him anything in the name of Jesus according to His word He will do it for you. He says if we know how to give good gifts to our children, how much more will your Father in Heaven give to His children that ask of Him. Ask Him today. Blessings, Blessings! Amen, and Amen.

PROMISES OF GOD

FATHER GOD ONLY HAS GOOD PLANS FOR YOU, FOR THE WORD OF GOD IS GOOD NEWS.

Jeremiah 29:11 (KJV) For I know the thought that I think toward you. saith the Lord, thoughts of peace, and not of evil, to give you an expected end.

Isaiah 40:31 (KJV) But they that wait upon the Lord shall renew their strength; they shall mount up with wings as eagles; they shall run, and not be weary; and they shall walk, and not faint.

Isaiah 48:17 (KJV) Thus saith the Lord, thy redeemer the Holy One of Israel; I am the Lord thy God which teacheth thee to profit, which leadeth thee by the way that thou shouldest go.

Isaiah 43:19-20 (KJV) Remember ye not the former things neither consider the things of old.

Behold I will do a new thing, now it shall spring forth; shall ye not know it? I will even make a way in the wilderness, and rivers in the desert.

Jeremiah 9:24 (AMPLIFIED) But let him (or her) glories glory in this: that he (or she) understands and knows Me personally and practically, directly discerning and recognizing My character), that I am the Lord. Who practices loving-kindness, judgment, and righteousness in the earth, for in these things I delight, says the Lord.

Corinthians 1:31 (AMPLIFIED) So then, as it is written, Let him(or she) who boasts and proudly rejoices and glories, boast and proudly rejoice and glory in the Lord.

SUMMARY

The Lord desires that you bear much fruit for Him in this earth. Be a Blessing to someone everyday. Show His loving kindness and His mercy and His grace in this lost and dying world. Show His goodness, and His joy, whatever you sow you will reap. He will bless you abundantly with His love and everywhere you put your feet is Holy Ground, claim the heathen for your inheritance. The Lord says and everything you put your hands to will prosper.

We serve a great big God with no limits and no boundaries on the Blessings. He wants to bestow on you. Seek His Kingdom first and His Righteousness and all these things will be added unto you.

He said you shall not lack for any good thing, you walk uprightly before Him. Also when He Blesses He adds no sorrow to it. His desire for you is that you prosper and be in health even as your soul prospers. He is an Almighty Good and Awesome God. Blessings, Blessings! Amen and Amen.

INHERITANCE

OUR HOLY COVENANT WITH GOD AND EVERYTHING YOU HAVE INHERITED THROUGH HIM.

Jeremiah 31:3 (KJV) The Lord hath appeared of old unto me, saying, Yea, I have loved thee with an everlasting love therefore with loving kindness have I drawn thee.

Jeremiah 29:11-13 (KJV) For know the thoughts that I think toward you, saith the Lord, thoughts of peace, and not of evil, to give you an expected end. Then shall we call upon Me, and ye shall go and pray unto Me, and I will hearken unto you. And ye shall seek Me: and find Me, when ye shall search for Me with all your heart.

Jeremiah 43:1 -2 (KVJ) Fear not, for I have redeemed thee, I have called thee by thy name; thou art Mine. When thou pass through the waters, I will be with thee; and through the rivers, they shall not overflow thee; when thou walkest through the fire, thou shalt not be burned; neither shall the flame kindle upon thee.

SUMMARY

The Lord has made a Holy Covenant with His people. The blood covenant where everything we need is in the blood. You don't have to be sick anymore or poor anymore, or depressed or oppressed, by the devil. He has redeemed you from the curse of the law of sin and (spiritual) death because He became a curse for us when He hung on that cross. The blessings of Abraham should be flowing in our lives and He wasn't sick and he wasn't poor.

The Lord told him be fruitful and multiply and your descendants shall be as the sand by the seashore. So say Lord I receive the Blessings of Abraham now in Jesus Name. Blessings, Blessings! Amen and Amen.

THE KINGDOM OF GOD

IS HERE AMONG YOU AND HIS WILL, WILL BE DONE ON EARTH AS IT IS IN HEAVEN, THROUGH YOU HIS PRECIOUS DAUGHTER.

JESUS SPEAKING TO YOU

Luke 12:32 (KJV) Fear not, little flock; for it is your Father's good pleasure to give you the Kingdom.

Luke 9:55-56 (KJV) Ye know not what manner of spirit ye are of. For the Son of Man is not come to destroy men's lives, but to save them.

Matthew 25: 34 (KJV) Then shall the King say unto them on His right hand, Come, ye blessed of My Father, inherit the kingdom prepared for you from the foundation of the world.

SUMMARY

It is your Heavenly Father's good pleasure for you to walk in your inheritance and your Kingdom authority. The Kingdom of God is Righteousness, Joy and Peace in the Holy Ghost and the Glory of God is all God has and all God is, and when you come to Jesus, the Kingdom of Heaven is yours through Him. Then you become His Ambassador and you are representing Him on this earth right now, and all that you need is in Him.Blessings, Blessings! Amen and Amen.

EPILOGUE FORTHE COLOR PURPLE

With the color Purple you have seen why they put the purple drape over the Cross at Easter time, because He is royalty. He is the King of Kings and the Lord of Lords. He rules and reigns with all authority in Heaven and in earth and when you come into His kingdom, you have the same authority in His name. You have now become royalty you have become a peculiar person, because you have entered a new supernatural realm. You have now become the daughter of the Most High God. You don't need to hang your head down in shame and guilt; He took all that for you.

You can walk with your head held high knowing who your big brother is and what He has done for you that. You are His Queen in His Kingdom and you worship His Majesty. You have dominion in His name to rule on this earth for His Glory. You have also His Inheritance, His Promises, He is your Mediator, and He intercedes for you constantly. Walk in your inheritance and never be ashamed of your King because there is none higher or any that can compare to Him. All Spiritual Blessings in Heavenly Places right now abound in your life now and forevermore.

4

BLUE

REVEALED WILL OF GOD (PROPHETIC) PRIESTHOOD, SEATED WITH THE LORD IN HEAVENLY PLACES, HEAVENLY LOVE, THE HOLY SPIRIT, AUTHORITY, WASHING OF THE WATER OF THE WORD. GRACE OVERCOMER, THE TRUTH, MESSIAH, THE RIVER OF GOD.

Scriptures where the color blue is mentioned in the Bible:

Exodus 24:10 (KJV) And they saw the God of Israel; and there was under His Feet as it were a paved work of a Sapphire Stone, and as it were the body of Heaven in His Clearness.

Ezekiel 1:26 (KJV) And above the firmament that was over their head was the likeness of a throne, as the appearance of a Sapphire Stone; and upon the likeness of the throne was the likeness as the appearance of a man above upon it.

Exodus 28:6 (NLT) The Craftsmen must make the Ephod of finely woven linen and skillfully embroider it with gold and with Blue, purple, and scarlet thread.

Scriptures that pertain to the color blue when you wear it:

BORN AGAIN

YOUR SPIRIT BEING MADE ALIVE UNTO GOD

John 3:5-8 (KJV) Jesus answered, verily, verily I say unto thee, Except a man (or woman) be born of the water and of the Spirit, he(or she) cannot enter into the kingdom of God. That which is born of flesh is flesh; and that which is born of the Spirit is Spirit. Marvel not that I said unto thee. Ye must be born-again. The wind bloweth where it listeneth, and thou hearest the sound thereof, but cannot tell whence it cometh, and whiter it goeth; so is every one that is born of the Spirit.

SUMMARY

Man and woman are made of Spirit, Soul and Body and when our spirit is not alive unto God we are spiritually dead. We will always be searching for something to fill us but nothing can fill us, men cannot fill us, always trying something new cannot fill us, only Jesus can fill that emptiness inside our hearts. Call on Him today and let Him fill you to overflowing with His Spirit.

REVEALED WILL OF GOD

BRINGING DOWN WALLS, OBSTACLES AND MOUNTAINS, IN YOUR LIFE (PROPHETIC) THAT SEEM INSUMOUNTABLE.

Philippians 2:13 (AMPLIFIED) (Not in your own strength) for it is God Who is all the while effectually at work in you (energizing and creating in you the power and desire), both to will and to work for His good pleasure and satisfaction and delight.

1 Thessalonians 5 12-23 (KJV) And we beseech you, brethren, to know them which labor among you and are over you in the Lord, and admonish you; And to esteem them very highly in love for their work's sake. And be at peace among yourselves. Now we exhort you, brethren, warn them that are unruly, comfort the feebleminded, support the weak, and be patient toward all men (or women). See that none render evil for evil unto any man (or woman); but follow that which is good, both among yourselves, and to all men (or women).

Rejoice evermore. Pray without ceasing. In everything give thanks: for this is the will of God in Christ Jesus concerning you. Quench not the Spirit.

Despise not prophesying. Prove all things; hold fast that which is good. Abstain from all appearance of evil. And the very God of peace sanctify you wholly; and I pray God your whole spirit and soul and body be preserved blameless unto the coming of our Lord Jesus Christ.

Joshua 1:8 (KJV) This book of the law shall not depart out of thy mouth, but thou shalt meditate therein day and night, that thou mayest observe to do according to all that is written therein; for then thou shalt make thy way prosperous, and then thou shalt have good success.

Matthew 6:10 (KJV) Thy kingdom come. Thy will be done in earth, as it is in heaven.

Ephesians 1:9 (AMPLIFIED) Making known to us the mystery (secret) of His will (of His plan, of His purpose). [And it is this] In accordance with His good pleasure (His merciful intention) which He had previously purposed and set forth in Him.

SUMMARY

Jesus is saying to meditate which means to mutter out loud the word of God get it in your spirit. To know how much He loves you and all His promises to you. They shall come to pass in your life the word says as it is in Heaven it shall be done in Earth. You can have Heaven on Earth, yes we go through trials and tribulations but we have the victory in all of them through Jesus. So we are to admonish one another be as servants to one another, love one another in the love of Jesus. Jesus said in the world you shall have tribulation but be of good cheer for I have overcome the world, and your faith is the victory that overcomes the world. He said my peace I give unto you, not as the world gives you, the Joy of the Lord is your strength. Overflow of Blessings!!!

PRIESTHOOD

JESUS HAS CALLED US AS PRIESTS AND KINGS, UNTO GOD YOU ARE ALREADY ORDAINED BY GOD.

1 Peter 2:5 (AMPLIFIED) (Come) and, like living stones, be yourselves built (into) a spiritual house, for a Holy (dedicated, consecrated) priesthood, to offer up (those) spiritual sacrifices (that are) acceptable and pleasing to God through Jesus Christ.

1 Peter 2:9 (AMPLIFIED) But you arc a chosen race, a royal priesthood, a dedicated nation,(God's) own purchased, special people, that you may set forth the wonderful deeds and display the virtues and perfections of Him Who called you out of darkness into His Marvelous Light.

Exodus 19:5-6 (AMPLIFIED) Now therefore, if you will obey My voice in Truth and keep My Covenant, then you shall be My own Peculiar Possession and Treasure from among and above all peoples; for all the earth is Mine. And you shall be to Me a Kingdom of Priests, a Holy Nation (consecrated, set apart to the Worship of God). These are the words you shall speak to the Israelites.

Hebrews 7:26 (KJV) For such an High Priest became us, who is Holy, Harmless, Undefiled, separate from sinners, and made higher than the Heavens.

Hebrews 9:11-12 (KJV) But Christ being come an High Priest of good things to come, by a greater and more Perfect Tabernacle, not made with hands, that is to say, not of this building; Neither by the blood of goats and calves, but by His own Blood He entered in once into the Holy Place.

Having obtained Eternal Redemption for you, Jesus became your High Priest when He shed His Blood, for you and me and the whole world at the Cross. Now when you accept that Precious Blood every drop that was offered up as a sacrifice, you have become one of His Priests, to show forth the praises of Him. Who took you for Himself and laid His life down and took all the shame, for the Joy that was set before Him and that is you. Bless You Abundantly Amen and Amen.

SEATED WITH THE LORD IN HEAVENLY PLACES YOUR POSITION IN CHRIST, YOU ARE SEATED WITH HIM IN YOUR SPIRIT MAN IN HEAVENLY PLACES.

Ephesians 1:3 (KJV) Blessed be the God and Father of our Lord Jesus Christ, who hath blessed us with all Spiritual Blessings in Heavenly Places in Christ.

Ephesians 2:5-6 (KJV) Even when we were dead in sins, hath quickened us together with Christ, (by grace ye are saved.) And hath raised us up together, made us sit together in Heavenly Places in Christ Jesus.

Hebrews 3:1 (AMPLIFIED) So Then, brethren, consecrated and set apart for God, who share in the Heavenly calling, (thoughtfully and attentively) consider Jesus, the Apostle and High Priest Whom we confessed (as ours when we embraced the Christian faith)

SUMMARY

Spiritually you are seated with Christ. You have access the Throne of God right now, through Jesus and the Blood that is on the Mercy Seat for you. You can come Boldly before His Throne Room, in the time of need. He ever liveth to make intercession for you, and through Him you have all the Rights and Privileges that Jesus gave you when He died at Calvary on the Cross.

He said all Power in Heaven and on Earth has been given to Him. Through His Name and His Blood has been given to you. He commanded you to exercise that power as His Body of Believers. Be Saved, Healed and Free in Jesus Name. Amen and Amen.

HEAVENLY LOVE

THE PURE AND HOLY LOVE OF JESUS, WITHOUT ANY SPOT OR WRINKLE, FOR HE IS LOVE THAT IS HIS WHOLE PERSON.

Ephesians 1:4 (AMPLIFIED) Even as (in His Love) He chose us (actually picked us out for Himself as His own) in Christ before the foundation of the world that we should be Holy (Consecrated and set apart for Him) and blameless in His sight, even above reproach, before Him in Love.

Corinthians 13:4-8 (AMPLIFIED) Love endures long and is patient and kind; love never is envious nor boils over with jealousy, is not boastful or vainglorious, does not display itself haughtily. It is not conceited (arrogant and inflated with pride); it is not rude (unmannerly) and does not act unbecomingly. Love (God's love in us) does not insist on its own rights or its own way, for it is not self-seeking; it is not touchy or resentful; it takes no account of the evil done to it (it pays no attention to a suffered wrong). It does not rejoice at injustice and unrighteousness, but rejoices when right and truth prevail.

Love bears up under anything and everything that comes is ever ready to believe the best of every person, its hopes are fadeless under all circumstances, and it endures everything (without weakening). Love never fails (never fades out or becomes obsolete or comes to an end).

Deuteronomy 6:5-6 (KJV) And thou shalt love the Lord thy God with all thine heart, and with all thy soul and with all thy might.

Matthew 19:19 (KJV) Honor thy Father and thy Mother: and, thou shalt love thy neighbor as thyself.

John 13:34 (KJV) A new commandment I give unto you. That ye love one another: as 1 have loved you, that ye also love one another. And these words, which I command thee this day, shall be in thine heart.

John 15:16-17 (KJV) Ye have not chosen me, but I have chosen you, and ordained you, that ye should go and bring forth fruit, and that your fruit should remain: that whatsoever ye shall ask of the Father in my name. He may give it to you. These things I command you, that ye love one another

SUMMARY

Jesus love for us never fails, you or come to an end, man (or woman) can fail you but Jesus is always there with His love, Saying come to me all who are heavy laden and I will give you rest for your soul. My peace in the midst of you circumstances and I will lead and guide you, by my spirit into Green Pastures and Quiet Still Waters. That means to seek Peace in your life at all costs and pursue it. That you may live a Peaceful life .

THE HOLY SPIRIT

THE HOLY SPIRITS WORK IN YOUR LIFE, HE IS THE ONLY PERSON YOU HAVE TO PLEASE. HE IS YOUR HELPER, COMFORTER, AND GUIDES YOU INTO ALL TRUTH. HE ALSO IS THE ONLY PERSON THAT KNOWS ALL YOUR WEAKNESSES, AND STILL IS CONTENT WITH YOU.

John 14:26-27 (KJV) But the Comforter, which is the Holy Ghost, whom the Father will send in my Name, He shall teach you all things, and bring all things to your remembrance whatsoever I have said unto you. Peace I leave with you, My Peace I give unto you: not as the world liveth, give I unto you. Let not your heart be troubled, neither let it be afraid.

Ephesians 1:13 (KJV) In whom ye also trusted, after that ye heard the word of Truth; the Gospel of your Salvation; in whom also after that ye believed, ye were sealed with that Holy Spirit of Promise.

Ephesians 4:20 (AMPLIFIED) And do not grieve the Holy Spirit of God (do not offend or vex or sadden Him), by Whom you were sealed (marked), branded as God's own, secured) for the day of redemption (of final deliverance through Christ from evil and the consequences of sin).

SUMMARY

The Sweet Precious Holy Spirit is there to lead and guide you into all Truth to help you in every situation in this life. To show you which way you should go. He will give you Peace in the middle of the storm, when you feel that you are being tossed to and fro. He will show you how to get to dry land, a safe place. He will quicken the word of God to you; one word from God will change your life, in a moment forever. Ask for His help for He is your Helper in the time of need, and a present help in the time of trouble. May the Blessings of the Lord abound on you and your family.

AUTHORITY

KNOWING THE POWER WE HAVE IN THE NAME OF JESUS. JESUS SPEAKING TO YOU

Luke 10:19 (AMPLIFIED) Behold! I have given you Authority and Power to trample upon serpents and scorpions, and (physical and mental strength and ability) over all the power that the enemy (possesses); and nothing shall in any way harm you.

Titus 2:15 (AMPLIFIED) Tell (them all) these things. Urge (advise, encourage, warn) and rebuke with full authority. Let no one despise or disregard or think little of you (conduct yourself and your teaching so as to command respect.

SUMMARY

Jesus is saying all power in Heaven and Earth has been given to Him and in His Name you have power over. All the power of the enemy (satan) you are to resist him in Jesus Name and with His Blood and he hast to flee from you.

You need to take your Authority in Jesus Name to take back whatever (satan) he has stolen from you. Rebuke him and tell him to take his hands off of your family, your health, your finances because he has no legal right if you are a child of the King to mess with anything that belongs to you. In Jesus Mighty, Holy Name. Amen and Amen.

WASHING OF THE WATER OF THE WORD

THE WORD OF GOD WILL CLEANSE YOU AND MAKE YOU WHITER THEN SNOW.

Ephesians 5:26 (AMPLIFIED) So that He might sanctify her, having cleansed her by the Washing of Water with the Word.

Titus 3:5 (KJV) Not by works of Righteousness which we have done, but according to His Mercy He Saved us, by the Washing of Regeneration, and renewing of the Holy Ghost.

Hebrews 10:22 (KJV) Let us draw near with a true heart in full assurance of faith, having our hearts sprinkled from an evil conscience, and our bodies washed with pure water.

Deuteronomy 8:3 (KJV) And He humbled thee, and suffered thee to hunger, and fed thee with manna, which thou knowest not, neither did thy fathers know; that he might make thee know that man (or woman) doth not live by bread only, but by every word that procedeth out of the mouth of the Lord doth man (or woman) live.

Psalm 119:11 (KJV) Thy word have I hid in mine heart, that I might not sin against thee.

Psalm 119:105 (KJV) Thy word is a lamp unto my feet, and a light unto my path.

Isaiah 40:8 (KJV) The grass withereth, the flower fadeth: but the word of our God shall stand for ever.

John 17:17 (KJV) Sanctify them through thy truth: thy word is truth.

Hebrews 4:12 (KJV) For the Word of God is Quick, and Powerful. And Sharper than any two edged sword, piercing even to the dividing Asunder of Soul and Spirit, and of the joints and marrow, and is s Discerner of the thoughts and intents of the heart.

Peter 1:25 (AMPLIFIED) But the Word of the Lord (divine instruction, the Gospel) endures forever. And this Word is the good news which was preached to you.

SUMMARY

Jesus is the Word of God and He will get rid of anything in your life that does not belong there if you let Him. He loves you too much to leave you the way you were. He only wants the best for you and He is the Best. He is Lord of all so let His Word Cleanse you and Wash you continually as you walk with Him in this journey in this life. Bless you Abundantly Amen and Amen.

GOD'S GRACE

GOD'S UMERITED FAVOR ON YOU EVEN THROUGH YOU DON'T DESERVE IT.

Psalms 84:11 (AMPLIFIED) For the Lord God is a Sun and Shield; the Lord bestows (present) grace and favor and (future) glory (honor, splendor, and heavenly bliss! No good thing will He withhold from those who walk uprightly.

Proverbs 3:34 (AMPLIFIED) Though He scoffs at the scoffers and scorns the scorners, yet He gives His undeserved favor to the low (in rank), the humble, and the afflicted.

James 4:6 (AMPLIFIED) But He gives more and more grace (a power of the Holy Spirit, to meet this evil tendency and all others fully). That is why He says, God sets Himself against the proud and haughty, but gives grace (continually) to the lowly (those who are humble enough to receive it).

Romans 3:24 (KJV) Being justified freely by His grace through the redemption that is in Christ Jesus.

Romans 5:20 (KJV) Moreover the law entered, that the offence might abound. But where sin abounded, grace did much more abound.

Romans 6:14 (AMPLIFIED) For sin shall not (any longer) exert dominion over you, since now you are not under Law (as slaves), but under grace (as subjects of God's favor and mercy).

Corinthians 12:9(AMPLIFIED) But He said to me. My grace (my favor and loving-kindness and mercy) is enough for you (sufficient against any danger and enables you to bear the trouble manfully): for My strength and power are made perfect (fulfilled and completed) and show themselves most effective in (your) weakness. Therefore, I will all the more gladly glory in my weaknesses and infirmities, that the strength and power of Christ (the Messiah) may rest (yes, may pitch a tent over and dwell) upon me!

Ephesians 2:5 (KJV) Even when we were dead in sins, hath quickened us together with Christ, (by grace ye are saved).

SUMMARY

Grace is God's favor even though you don't deserve it. His grace and His mercies are new every morning. Great is His faithfulness. So rejoice for you are not under the law anymore but under His Awesome Grace. There is therefore now no condemnation. to you who under Grace, but the conviction of the Holy Spirit (when we are offending Him).

For we are called according to His Purpose and Plan to live a Holy Life before Him. Then we don't want to grieve the Holy Spirit, listen to that inner voice, most of the time it is a still small voice. Then you can't lose. Blessings, Blessings, Amen and Amen

OVERCOMER

JESUS HAS OVERCOME THE DEVIL BY HIS BLOOD, AND BY HIS WORDS, AND THAT IS THE SAME FOR YOU TODAY.

JESUS SPEAKING TO YOU

Revelation 3:19-21 (AMPLIFIED) Those whom I (dearly and tenderly) love, I tell their faults and convict and reprove and chasten (1 discipline and instruct them). So be enthusiastic and in earnest and burning with zeal and repent (changing your mind and attitude). Behold I stand at the door and knock; if anyone hears and listens to and heeds My voice and opens the door, I will come in to him (or her), and will cat with him (or her) and He (or she) (will eat) with Me. He (or she) who overcomes (is victorious), I will grant him (or her) to sit beside Me on My Throne as I myself overcame (was victorious) and sat down beside My Father on His Throne.

Revelation 1:17-18 (KJV) Fear not; I am the first and the last. I am He that liveth, and was dead; and, behold, I am alive for evermore Amen; and have the keys of hell and of death.

Galatians 3:13 (KJV) Christ hath redeemed us from the curse of the law, being made a curse for us: for it is written. Cursed is every one that hangeth on a tree. That the Blessing of Abraham might come on the Gentiles through Jesus Christ; that we might receive the promise of the Spirit through faith.

SUMMARY

In Christ you have the victory and the Lord said you overcome by the Blood of the Lamb and the word of your testimony. Tell everyone what the Lord has done for you and how good He has been to you even though you did not deserve it.

Tell everyone of His Mercy and Grace and how it covers you everyday. You are to plead His Blood over you and every situation you are facing today and will ever face in this life. Call on His Name Jesus, Jesus because the devil cannot penetrate through Jesus Blood or His Name. Resist the devil and he will flee from you. Jesus is the Alpha and the Omega, the beginning and the end, He is your very present help in the time of trouble, and He is Risen from the dead and is alive forevermore. Use His Name and His Blood.

THE TRUTH

JESUS SAID I AM THE WAY, THE TRUTH, AND THE LIGHT AND NO MAN OR WOMAN, COMES TO THE FATHER BUT THROUGH HIM.

Psalms 25:4-5 (AMPLIFIED) Show me thy ways, O Lord; teach me thy paths. Guide me in Your truth and faithfulness. Teach me, for You are the God of my salvation; for You (You only and altogether) do I wait (expectantly) all the day long.

Psalm 91:4 (AMPLIFIED) (Then) He will cover you with His pinions, and under His wings shall you trust and find refuge: His truth and His faithfulness are a shield and a buckler.

Psalm 117:2 (KJV) For his merciful kindness is great toward us: and the truth of the Lord endureth for ever. Praise ye the Lord.

Proverbs 16:6 (KJV) By mercy and truth iniquity is purged: and by the fear of the Lord men (or women) depart from evil.

John 1:14 (KJV) And the Word was made flesh, and dwelt among us, (and we beheld his glory, the glory as of the only begotten of the Father full of grace and truth.

John 8:32 (KJV) And ye shall know the truth, and the truth shall make you free.

JESUS SPEAKING TO YOU

John 14:6 (KJV) Jesus saith unto him I am the way, the truth, and the life: no man (or woman) cometh unto the Father, but by me.

Ephesians 4:21 (AMPLIFIED) Assuming that you have really heard Him and been taught by Him, as (all) Truth is in Jesus (embodied and personified in Him).

2 Thessalonians 2:10 (KJV) And with all deceivableness of unrighteousness in them that perish; because they received not the love of the truth, that they might be saved.

John 18:37 (AMPLIFIED) Pilate said to Him. Then You are a King? Jesus answered, You say it! [You speak correctly] For I am a King. [Certainly I am a King!] This is why I was born, and for this I have come into the world, to bear witness to the Truth. Everyone who is of the Truth [who is a friend of the Truth, who belongs to the Truth] hears and listens to My voice.

SUMMARY

Jesus came into this world to bear witness to the Truth for He is the Truth. He said if you listen to His word for He is the word made flesh, then you will know how to live this life for Him. You will not be confused or scattered by every wind of doctrine that is available to you. You cannot serve two masters you cannot serve God and Mammon, which is the world.

The world's ways are in contrary or total opposition to Him and His word. The Lord said My ways are higher then your ways, I know what is best for you, I want to protect you from evil and against anything that will try to harm you, if you listen and obey I will show you the path of life, and give you the right road to take so you will not fall into a ditch, and you will find me when you seek me with your whole heart.

When you call on me I will answer you I will not turn away. For I am the God of more then enough, I have already known you before the foundation of the world. I have called you by name. I am your Heavenly Father and I will in no way cast you out or reject you I am just waiting to pour My love on you and I only have good things for you, for I am a Good God. Blessings, Blessings!!! Amen and Amen.

MESSIAH

JESUS IS THE LORD AND SAVIOR OF THIS WORLD, HE IS THE ANOINTED ONE THE HOLY ONE OF ISAREL

Ephesians 4:15 (AMPLIFIED) Rather, let our lives lovingly express truth [in all things, speaking truly, dealing truly, living truly). Enfolded in love, let us grow up in every way and all things unto Him Who is the Head, [even] Christ (the Messiah, the Anointed One).

Hebrews 9:15 (AMPLIFIED) (Christ the Messiah) is therefore the Negotiator and Mediator of an (entirely) new agreement (testament covenant), so that those who are called and offered it may receive the fulfillment of the promised everlasting inheritance— since a death has taken place which rescues and delivers and redeems them from the transgressions committed under the (old) first agreement.

SUMMARY

Jesus is the mediator between God and Man (or woman). He intercedes for His believers and says to the Father not guilty and when the Father looks on you He only sees the Blood of Jesus. He doesn't see your sin anymore He has put it into the sea of forgetfulness never to be remembered anymore, because you serve a Holy, Holy, God He is the Messiah. The Lord and Savior and Redeemer, the Lamb of God who took away the sins of this world. Who is and was and is to come with the shout of triumph.

Rejoice, Rejoice, for you sin debt has been paid forevermore. Rejoice, Rejoice in the Lord for He is good and His mercy endures forever. May His Blessings overtake you today and everyday because He daily loadeth you down with benefits so expect good and great things everyday. Blessings, Blessings! Amen and Amen.

THE RIVER OF GOD

GOD'S WORD BRINGS PEACE AND RIGHTEOUSNESS AND IS A RIVER OF LIVING WATER IN A DRY AND THIRSTY LAND

Isaiah 48:18 (AMPLIFIED) Oh, that you had hearkened to my commandments! Then your peace and prosperity would have been like a flowing river, and your righteousness [the holiness and purity of the nation] like the [abundant] waves of the sea.

Isaiah 66:12 (AMPLIFIED) For thus says the Lord: Behold, I will extend peace to her like a river, and the glory of the nations like an overflowing stream; then you will be nursed, you will be carried on her hip and trotted [lovingly bounced up and down] on her [God's maternal] knee

John 7:38 (AMPLIFIED) He who believes in Me [who cleaves to and trusts in and relies on Me] as the Scripture has said, From his innermost being shall flow [continuously] springs and rivers of living water.

SUMMAERY

Jesus said out your belly shall flow rivers of living water. That means out of your spiritual heart shall come the washing of the water of the word to remove impurities and unholiness from your inner being. The word is a river refreshing, renewing and restoring you to His image and after His likeness. Itmakes you every bit whole, lifting your spirit man (or woman) up. He is constantly working His will in your life. He loves you to much to leave you the way He found you. He is making you into a vessel of honor for His Glory which is all God has and all He is for His purpose and plan for you.

You were created for His Glory to Worship and Praise Him and let your life be a living testimony of His goodness, His grace. Let your life and example and your praise show forth to glorify your Father in Heaven, tell the Lord how grateful you are to Him, and how much you love Him .Jesus and the Sweet Precious Holy Spirit who is always there to guide and direct you footsteps, to keep you from stumbling and falling. If you do He is always there to pick you up and to tell you. That you can do it and you can make it.

Quitters don't win and winners don't quit. To please the Lord is to walk by faith by being obedient to His word, and what He tells you to do, listen to the Spirit of God not to man (or woman's) natural reasoning. Bless you with rivers of Blessings!!!

EPILOGUE FOR THE COLOR BLUE:

You have seen in this chapter the powerful meanings of the color Blue, and how it relates to you in your daily living. In the Old Testament the priest wore a prayer shawl in the temple which consisted of White and Gold and Blue. After you finish this book you will know why the Lord wanted those colors of White and Blue on it.

You will also see on a clear day why the sky is Blue and White that covers the earth, because it is His will for His word to be established not only in Heaven but in earth, to wash the earth clean from the fallen Adamic nature when Adam fell, Christ became the second Adam redeeming all mankind and womankind, redeeming the world back to Himself.

You might say then, why are all these evil things going on in the world today, because God will never violate your will it is your choice who you will serve. If you follow the flesh you will fulfill the lusts of the flesh but if you follow after the Holy Spirit you will not fulfill the lust of your flesh. Walk in the spirit today give life to someone, the life of Jesus. Be Blessed and follow that spirit of truth in you.

5

WHITE

THE BRIDE OF CHRIST, PURITY, SURRENDER, LIGHT,ANGELS,THE SAINTS,PEACE,VICTORY,THE CREATOR, INNOCENCE,SPIRITUAL AGE,PERFECTION,SALVATION,JOY,FESTIVE REJOICING, GLORY

Scriptures where the color White is mentioned in the Bible:

Daniel 7:9 (KJV) I beheld till the thrones were cast down, and the Ancient of days did sit, whose garment was white as snow, and the hair of his head like the pure wool: his throne was like the fiery flame and his wheels as burning fire.

Revelation 3:4-5 (KJV) Thou hast a few names even in Sardis which have not defiled their garments; and they shall walk with me in white: for they are worthy. He that overcometh, the same shall be clothed in white raiment; and I will not blot out his name out of the book of life, but I will confess his name before my Father, and before his angels.

Revelation 4:4 (KJV) And round about the throne were four and twenty seats: and upon the seats I saw four and twenty elders sitting, clothed in white raiment; and they had on their heads crowns of gold.

Revelation 6:2 (KJV) And I saw, and behold a white horse: and he that sat on him had a bow; and a crown was given unto him: and he went forth conquering, and to conquer.

Revelation 19:14 (KJV) And the armies which were in heaven followed him upon white horses, clothed in fine linen, white and clean. Scriptures that pertain to the color White when you wear it:

THE BRIDE OF CHRIST

JESUS IS COMING BACK FOR A VICTORIOUS CHURCH, WITHOUT SPOT OR WRINKLE A HOLY TABERNACLE.

Isaiah 61:10 (KJV) I will greatly rejoice in the LORD, my soul shall be joyful in, he hath covered me with the robe of righteousness, as a bridegroom decketh himself with ornaments, and as a bride adorneth herself with her jewels.

Revelation 21:2 (KJV) And he carried me away in the spirit to a great and high mountain, and showed me that great city, the holy Jerusalem, descending out of heaven from God.

Isaiah 62:5 (KJV) For as a young man marrieth a virgin, so shall thy sons marry thee: and as the bridegroom rejoiceth over the bride, so shall thy God rejoice over thee.

SUMMARY

Jesus is coming soon are you ready to meet Him in the air? He will descend from Heaven with a shout of triumph and you will ascend to meet the King of Kings and Lord of Lords. As His believers we are His church and His bride and you will see Him in all of His Glory, so be one of the five wise virgins who had their lamp lit. Be prepared for your beautiful Lord and Savior. Have your life in order. Live a holy and blameless life before Him. Blessings, Blessings! Amen and Amen.

PURITY

THE WAYS OF THE LORD ARE PURE AND HOLY, AND HE SAID THAT YOU SHOULD LIVE A HOLY AND PURE LIFE ALSO BEFORE HIM.

Psalms 12:6 (KJV) The words of the LORD are pure words: as silver tried in a furnace of earth, purified seven times.

Psalms 19:8 (AMPLIFIED) The precepts of the Lord are right, rejoicing the heart; the commandment of the Lord is pure and bright, enlightening the eyes.

Psalms 24:4-5 (AMPLIFIED) He who has clean hands and a pure heart, who has not lifted himself up to falsehood or to what is false, nor sworn deceitfully.5 He shall receive blessing from the Lord and righteousness from the God of his Salvation.

Proverbs 15:26 (KJV) The thoughts of the wicked are an abomination to the LORD: but the words of the pure are pleasant words.

Proverbs 30:5 (KJV) Every word of God is pure: he is a shield unto them that put their trust in him.

SUMMARY

You, therefore, serve a Holy and Pure God without spot or wrinkle. He said, "be ye Holy as I am Holy". Abstain yourself from worldly lusts of the flesh. Keep your heart and mind pure before me. Fill yourself with my word daily. Let the intentions of your heart and the words of your mouth be acceptable to the Lord. As you keep renewing yourself with the word of God, the things of this world will grow slowly dim in the light of His Glory and Grace.

Keep your heart on whatever things are Pure, Holy, True, Honest and of Good Report; then in times of trouble you will know it is a testing of your faith. You will know not to focus on the circumstances but the word of God. That is what should be coming out of your mouth. Walk in His love, and then and only then will you see things turn completely around for His Glory. The Lord will show Himself strong on your behalf. Blessings, Blessings!!! Amen and Amen

SURRENDER

WITHOUT THE LORD YOU CAN DO NOTHING, BUT WITH HIM ALL THINGS ARE POSSIBLE, IF YOU SURRENDER YOUR LIFE TO HIM. MAKE HIM YOUR MASTER AND THE LORD OF YOUR LIFE.

Acts 17:28 (KJV) For in him we live, and move, and have our being; as certain also of your own poets have said, For we are also his offspring.

Psalms 23:6 (AMPLIFIED) Surely or only goodness, mercy, and unfailing love shall follow me all the days of my life, and through the length of my days the house of the Lord [and His presence] shall be my dwelling place.

SUMMARY

So it is a total Surrender to the Lord of your spirit, soul and body. The benefits are out of this world. When you let the Holy Spirit lead and guide you everyday you can avoid a lot of pitfalls in your life. The Lord says obedience is better then sacrifice, even when your natural mind says you can't do that. God will take you a long way to fulfill His purpose and plan for your life. Surely goodness and mercy will follow you all the days of your life. You are highly favored with God and man (or woman). Right now speak it out, believe it and receive it today. Surrender all to Jesus.

LIGHT

JESUS IS THE LIGHT OF THIS WORLD, AND FOR ALL ETERNITY AND HIM THERE IS NO DARKNESS.

Psalms 4:6 (KJV) There be many that say, Who will show us any good? LORD, lift thou up the light of thy countenance upon us.

Psalms 36:9 (KJV) For with thee is the fountain of life: in thy light shall we see light.

Psalms 43:3 (KJV) O send out thy light and thy truth: let them lead me; let them bring me unto thy holy hill, and to thy tabernacles.

Psalms 119:105 (KJV) Thy word is a lamp unto my feet, and a Light unto my path.

Isaiah 5:20 (KJV) Woe unto them that call evil good, and good evil; that put darkness for light, and light for darkness; that put bitter for sweet, and sweet for bitter!

Isaiah 58:8 (AMPLIFIED) 8Then shall your light break forth like the morning, and your healing (your restoration and the power of a new life) shall spring forth speedily; your righteousness (your rightness, your justice, and your right relationship with God) shall go before you [conducting you to peace and prosperity], and the glory of the Lord shall be your rear guard.

Isaiah 60:1(AMPLIFIED) ARISE [from the depression and prostration in which circumstances have kept you—rise to a new life]! Shine (be radiant with the glory of the Lord), for your light has come, and the glory of the Lord has risen upon you!

Matthew 5:16 (KJV) Let your light so shine before men, that they may see your good works, and glorify your Father which is in heaven.

John 1:3-4 (KJV) All things were made by him; and without him was not any thing made that was made. In him was life; and the life was the light of men.

John 1:5 (AMPLIFIED) And the Light shines on in the darkness, for the darkness has never overpowered it [put it out or absorbed it or appropriated it, and is unreceptive to it].

John 1:7 (AMPLIFIED) This man came to witness, that he might testify of the Light, that all men might believe in it [adhere to it, trust it, and rely upon it] through him.

John 1:9 (AMPLIFIED) There it was—the true Light [was then] coming into the world [the genuine, perfect, steadfast Light] that illumines every person.

John 8:12 (AMPLIFIED) Once more Jesus addressed the crowd. He said, I am the Light of the world. He who follows Me will not be walking in the dark, but will have the Light which is Life.

SUMMARY

Jesus is the Light of the world and the Light always overcomes the darkness. When you speak His word it pierces through to the heart of man. It changes their lives, it changes their hearts and you get stronger in the word. Lives will never be the same. In Jesus Name you are Blessed to be a Blessing Amen and Amen

ANGELS

MINISTERING SPIRITS SENT FORTH TO THE HEIRS OF SALVATION, TO BRING INTO EXISTENCE IN THIS EARTH THE WORD OF GOD, WHICH YOU SPEAK SO LET YOUR ANGELS GO TO WORK FOR YOU.

Psalms 34:7 (AMPLIFIED) The Angel of the Lord encamps around those, who fear Him [who revere and worship Him with awe] and each of them He delivers.

Psalms 103:20 (AMPLIFIED) Bless (affectionately, gratefully praise) the Lord, you His angels, you mighty ones who do His commandments, hearkening to the voice of His word.

Genesis 28:12 (KJV) And he (Jacob) dreamed that there was a ladder set up on the earth, and the top of it reached to heaven; and the Angels of God were ascending and descending on it!

Matthew 25:31 (KJ) When the Son of man shall come in His Glory; and all the Holy Angels with Him, then shall He sit upon the Throne of His Glory:

Luke 15:10 (AMPLIFIED) Even so, I tell you, there is joy among and in the presence of the Angels of God over one [especially] wicked person who repents (changes his mind for the better, heartily amending his ways, with abhorrence of his past sins).

John 1:51 (AMPLIFIED) Then He said to him, I assure you, most solemnly I tell you all, you shall see heaven opened, and the Angels of God ascending and descending upon the Son of Man.

Hebrews 13:29 (AMPLIFIED) Do not forget or neglect or refuse to extend hospitality to strangers (in the brotherhood being friendly, cordial; and gracious, sharing the comforts of your home and doing your part generously], for through it some have entertained Angels without knowing it.

SUMMARY

Angels are very important to a believer. There are the ministering spirits that go to work for you when you speak the word of God over people or over your circumstances. They are sent forth to bring it to pass. Speak the word and see how the Angels will work for you. Speak what God says not what the world says and your life will shine showing God's Glory in this earth. Blessings, Blessings! Amen and Amen.

SAINTS

BELIEVERS IN CHRIST, ARE STILL HIS DISCIPLES TODAY WHO ARE SET APART TO BE HOLY AND SANCTIFIED FOR HIS GLORY.

Psalms 97:10 (KJV) Ye that love the Lord, hate evil: He perserveth the souls of His Saints: He delivered them out of the hand of the wicked.

Romans 8:27 (AMPLIFIED) And He who searches the hearts of men (or women) knows what is in the mind of the [Holy Spirit] what His intent is], because the Spirit intercedes and pleads [before God] in behalf of the Saints according to and in harmony with God's will.

1 Corinthians 6:2 (AMPLIFIED) Do you not know that the Saints (the Believers) will [one day] judge, and govern the world? And if the world (itself) is to be judged and ruled by you, are you unworthy and incompetent to try [such petty matters] of the smallest courts of justice?

Revelation 5:8 (KJV) And when he had taken the book, the four beasts and four and twenty elders fell down before the Lamb, having every one of them harps, and golden vials full of odors, which are the prayers of Saints.

Revelation 19:7-8 (KJV) Let us be glad and rejoice, and give honor to Him; for the marriage of the Lamb is come, and His wife hath made herself ready. And to her was granted that she should be arrayed in fine linen, clean and White; for the fine linen is the righteousness of Saints.

SUMMARY

You are part of the Body of Christ. You are a part of His Bride that He is coming back for soon. You are one of his Saints set apart to be Holy and Blameless in His sight.

You are to be prepared and be one of the five wise virgins doing what He has called you to do for His Kingdom and His Glory on this earth. The Lord said you are higher then the Angels. He is the head of His church but you are in His body.

Live your life as a testimony unto Him and keep your body, Pure and Holy in His sight. For your redemption draweth nigh. Then He can say well done my good and faithful servant. Be ready and be prepared for the coming of your Lord Jesus Christ. He is coming back in White, He is the Bridegroom of His Church. Blessings, Blessings Amen and Amen

PEACE

JESUS CAME AND TOOK YOUR PEACE FOR YOU, SO YOU CAN HAVE PEACE IN EVERY TEST AND AFFLICTION IN THIS LIFE.

Numbers 6:26 (AMPLIFIED) The Lord lift up His [approving] countenance upon you and give you Peace (tranquility of heart and life continually).

Psalms 34:14 (AMPLIFIED) Depart from evil and do good; seek, inquire for, and crave Peace and pursue (go after) it!

Psalms 122:6 (KJV) Pray for the Peace of Jerusalem: they shall prosper that love thee.

Proverbs 16:7 (KJV) When a man's (or woman's) ways please the Lord, He maketh even his (or her) enemies to be at Peace with him (or her).

Isaiah 26:3 (AMPLIFIED) You will guard him (or her) and keep him (or her) in perfect and constant Peace whose mind [both its inclination and its character] is stayed on You, because he (or she) commits himself (or herself) to You, leans on You, and hopes confidently in You.

Isaiah 57:19 (AMPLIFIED) Peace, Peace to him (or her) who is far off [both Jew and Gentile] and to him (or her) who is near! Says the Lord; I create the fruit of his (or her) lops, and I will heal him (or her) [make his (or her) lips blossom anew with speech in thankful praise].

Luke 2:14 (AMPLIFIED) Glory to God in the highest [heaven] and on earth Peace among men (or women) with whom He is well pleased men (or women) of goodwill, of His favor.

Romans 5:1 (AMPLIFIED) Therefore, since we are justified (" acquitted, declared righteous, and given a right standing with God) through faith, let us {grasp the fact that we] have [the peace of reconciliation to hold and to enjoy] Peace with God through our Lord Jesus Christ (the Messiah, the Anointed One).

Galatians 5:22 (AMPLIFIED) But the fruit of the [Holy] Spirit [the work which His presence within accomplishes] is love, joy (gladness). Peace, patience, even temper, forbearance, kindness, goodness (benevolence), and faithfulness.

SUMMARY

Jesus came to give you Peace when you are in the middle of the storm, the fire or the flood, but you are under the Precious Blood of the Lamb. He will guide you and protect you from harm He will make a way of escape for you and be with you leading you with His right hand going before you.

You can have Peace in the midst of your circumstances knowing God will make a way for you when there seems to be no way. Remember, He knows all things beginning to the end, and He knows what is going to happen before you do.

He knows the choices you will make before you make them He will show you the way out of the trial and when you continue with Him, He will use it for His Glory, so you can help other people in the same situation. He takes your mess and turns it into your message. You serve a mighty Good God, and with Him all things are possible. Praise His Holy Name. Amen and Amen

VICTORY

JESUS GAVE YOU THE VICTORY IN EVERYTHING THAT COMES AGAINST YOU IN THIS LIFE, IN HIM AND THROUGH HIS BLOOD, HIS NAME, AND THE WORD OF YOUR TESTIMONY.

Psalms 98:1-2 (KJV) O Sing unto the Lord a new song, for He hath done marvelous things: His right hand, and His holy arm, hath gotten Him the victory. The Lord hath made known His salvation; His righteousness hath He openly shown in the sight of the heathen.

1 Corinthians 15:57-58 (KJV) But thanks be to God, which giveth us the victory through our Lord Jesus Christ. Therefore, my beloved brethren, be ye steadfast, unmoveable, always abounding in the work of the Lord, forasmuch as ye know that your labor is not in vain in the Lord. **1 John 5:4-5 (AMPLIFIED)** For whatever is born of God is victorious over the world; and this is the victory that conquers the world, even our faith. Who is it that is victorious over {that conquers] the world but he who believes that Jesus is the Son of God [who adheres to, trusts in, and relies on that fact]?

SUMMARY

Jesus has given you the victory. He said you are in this world but you are not of this world. Remain faithful to Him. Be rooted and grounded in the word of God. So when He returns He will find faith in this earth well let Him find it in you. Remain being led by the Holy Spirit, who will always lead and guide you in His truth.

The Lord said be not conformed to this world, to their views, doctrines and their fears but be ye transformed by the constant renewing of your mind on the word of God which is your shield against the principalities and powers of this world, and also wicked spirits in high places. Walk in faith and walk in love, which also is the victory in this earth.

Love casts out all fear, and if you have fear, the Lord said then you have not been made perfect in the love of Jesus.

Love, Joy and Peace to you always! Amen and Amen.

CREATOR

GOD IS THE MAKER OF HEAVEN AND EARTH AND EVERYTHING WITHIN, HE IS THE CREATOR OF THIS VAST UNIVERSE HE SPOKE IT AND IT CAME TO PASS.

Isaiah 40:28-29 (KJV) Hast thou not known? Hast thou not heard, that the everlasting God, the Lord, the Creator of the ends of the earth, fainteth not, neither is weary? There is no searching of His understanding. He giveth power to the faint: and to them that have no might He increaseth strength.

Genesis 1:1 (AMPLIFIED) In The beginning God (prepared, formed, fashioned, and) Created the heavens and the earth.

Hebrews 11:3 (AMPLIFIED) By faith we understand that the worlds [during the successive ages] were framed (fashioned, put in order, and equipped for their intended purpose) by the word of God, so that what we see was not made out of things which are visible.

Isaiah 43:7 (KJV) Even every one that is called by my name: for I have Created him(or her) for my glory, I have formed him(or her); yea, I have made him(or her).

Colossians 1:76-17 (AMPLIFIED) For it was in Him that all things were Created, in heaven and on earth, things seen and things unseen, whether thrones, dominions, rulers, or authorities: all things were Created and exist through Him [by His service, intervention] and in an for Him. And He Himself existed before all things, and in Him all things consist (cohere are held together.

Colossians 3:10 (AMPLIFIED) And have clothed yourselves with the new {spiritual self], which is [ever in the process of being] renewed and remolded into [fuller and more perfect knowledge upon] knowledge after the image (the likeness) of Him who Created it.

Revelation 4:11 (KJV) Thou art worthy, O Lord, to receive glory and honor and power: for thou hast Created all things, and for thy pleasure they are and were Created.

SUMMARY

The Lord is the Creator of all things and without Him there would be nothing that was Created by Him and for Him. That means we are here for His purpose and His pleasure. He spoke the heavens and the earth into existence by His words and you are Creating your world everyday with your mouth.

The miracle is in your mouth and out of the abundance of your heart your mouth speaketh.

So put the word of God in your mouth, and when the devil comes to steal you faith and you are under pressure, you will be speaking the solution, not the problem. It will turn around! Create what you want in your life. You can do it and you can make it in Jesus name. Blessings, Blessings!!! Amen and Amen.

INNOCENCE

JESUS TOOK ALL YOUR SINS AT THE CROSS, AND HE EVER LIVES, TO MAKE INTERCESSION FOR HIS SAINTS.

Romans 3:24-25 (AMPLIFIED) [All are justified and made upright and in right standing with God, freely and gratuitously by His grace (His unmerited favor and mercy), through the redemption which is [provided] in Christ Jesus. Whom God put forward [before the eyes of all] as a mercy seat and

Propitiation by His Blood [the cleansing and life-giving sacrifice of atonement and reconciliation, to be received] through faith. This was to show God's righteousness, because in His divine forbearance He had passed over and ignored former sins without punishment.

John 4:10 (AMPLIFIED) He (or she) who does not love has not become acquainted with God [does not and never did know Him], for God is love. In this the love of God was made manifest (displayed) where we are concerned: in that God sent His Son, the only begotten or unique [Son]; into the world so that we might live through Him. In this is love: not that we loved God, but that He loved us and sent His Son to be the Propitiation (the atoning sacrifice) for our sins.

SUMMARY

Jesus took all your sins at the Cross and the only thing you would be guilty of is if you have not accepted His great love, for you that really would be the only sin you would be held accounted for. Once you accept the supreme sacrifice, that He gave for you then you have been taken out of darkness into His light.

He stands before the Father and when Satan accuses you, before the Father in the throne of grace, Jesus points to His blood on the mercy seat for you and says they are innocent Father, not guilty. Praise the Lord it doesn't get any better then that. Bless you and bask in His great love. Amen and Amen.

SPIRITUAL AGE

THE SAINTS OF GOD WILL RULE AND REIGN THIS EARTH, FOR A THOUSAND YEARS AFTER THE SECOND COMING OF JESUS.

Revelation 21:1-3 (KJV) AND I saw a new heaven and a new earth: for the first heaven and a new earth were passed away; and there was no more sea. And John saw the holy city, New Jerusalem, coming down from God out of heaven, prepared as a bride adorned for her husband. I heard a great voice out of heaven saying, Behold, the tabernacle of God is with men, and He will dwell with them, and they shall be His people, and God Himself shall be with them, and be their God.

Revelation 20:6 (AMPLIFIED) Blessed (happy, to be envied) and holy (spiritually whole, of unimpaired innocence and proved virtue) is the person who takes part (shares) in the first resurrection! Over them the second death exerts no power or authority, but they shall be ministers of God and of Christ (the Messiah), and they shall rule along with Him a thousand years.

Revelation 22:3-5 (AMPLIFIED) There shall no longer exist there anything that is accursed (detestable, foul, offensive, impure, hateful, or horrible). But the throne of God and of the Lamb shall be in it, and His servants shall worship Him [pay divine honors to Him and do Him holy service]. They shall see His face, and His name shall be on their foreheads. And there shall be no more night; they have no need for lamplight or sunlight, for the Lord God will illuminate them and be their light, and they shall reign [as kings] forever and ever (through the eternities of the eternities).

SUMMARY

So the Spiritual Age of the church, is as I believe when you rule and reign with the Lord and all the saints on the new earth, that the Lord will create and the word says that the Bride of Christ will judge the world. You will forever be with the Lord. And there also will be a New Jerusalem, God's Holy City and Nation Israel.

Isn't it wonderful how the Lord knew the beginning to the end and He still loves everybody, with an everlasting love. It is not His will that any should perish and be cast into hell. Hell was not made for people but for satan and his demons, but yet God cannot and will not violate anybody's will. That is the only time Jesus will cry at the final judgment when He has to say depart from me I never knew you. So accept His love today and live forever with Him. Bless You. Amen and Amen.

PERFECTION

JESUS GAVE YOU PERFECTION IN HIM, BECAUSE IT'S IN HIM YOU SHOULD NOW LIVE, MOVE AND HAVE YOUR BEING.

Hebrews 6:1 (AMPLIFIED) Therefore Let us go on and get past the elementary stage in the teachings and doctrine of Christ (the Messiah), advancing steadily toward the completeness and Perfection that belong to spiritual maturity. Let us not again be laying the foundation of repentance and abandonment of dead works (dead formalism) and of the faith [by which you turned] to God.

Psalms 18:7 (AMPLIFIED) The law of the Lord is Perfect, restoring the [whole] person; the testimony of the Lord is sure, making wise the simple. Matthew 5:48 (AMPLIFIED) You, therefore, must be Perfect [growing into complete maturity of godliness in mind and character, having reached the proper height of virtue and integrity], as your heavenly Father is Perfect.

Corinthians 12:9 (AMPLIFIED) But He said to me, My grace (My favor and loving-kindness and mercy) is enough for you [sufficient against any danger and enables you to bear the trouble manfully]; for My strength and power are made Perfect (fulfilled and completed) and show themselves most effective in [your] weakness. Therefore, I will all the more gladly glory in my weaknesses and infirmities, that the strength and power of Christ (the Messiah) may rest (yes, may pitch a tent over and dwell) upon me!

Colossians 1:28 (AMPLIFIED) Him we preach and proclaim warning and admonishing everyone and instructing everyone in all wisdom (comprehensive insight into the ways and purposes of God), that we may present every person mature (full-grown, fully initiated, complete, and Perfect) in Christ (the Anointed One).

Hebrews 13:21 (KJV) Make you Perfect in every good work to do His will, working in you that which is well-pleasing in His sight, through Jesus Christ; to whom be glory forever and ever. Amen.

SUMMARY

Jesus is working in you and the hope of Glory is constantly changing you and perfecting you into His image and His likeness so when people see you, they see Jesus in you, they see the Light and they know there is something different about you. They should be drawn to you, because you have what the world is looking for inside of you. You should be a shining example of His love, light and life everyday. You should be looking more like Him. Blessings, Blessings, Amen and Amen

SALVATION

JESUS IS THE LORD AND SAVIOR OF THIS WORLD, HE BECAME THE SECOND ADAM, FOR YOU AND TOOK BACK EVERYTHING THAT THE DEVIL STOLE.

Exodus 15:2 (AMPLIFIED) The Lord is my Strength and my Song, and He has become my Salvation; this is my God, and I will praise Him, my father's God, and I will exalt Him.

Psalms 3:8 (AMPLIFIED) Salvation belongs to the Lord; May Your blessing be upon Your people. Selah [pause, and calmly think of that]!

Psalms 27:1 (KJV) The Lord is my Light and my Salvation; whom shall I fear? The Lord is the strength of my life; of whom shall I be afraid?

Psalms 118:14 (AMPLIFIED) The Lord is my Strength and Song; and He has become my Salvation.

Psalms 149:4 (KJV) For the Lord taketh pleasure in His people: He will beautify the meek with Salvation.

Isaiah 12:2 (KJV) Behold, God is my Salvation; I will trust, and not be afraid: for the Lord Jehovah is my strength and my song; He also is become my Salvation.

Isaiah 52:10 (AMPLIFIED) The Lord has made bare His holy arm before the eyes of all the nations [revealing Himself as the One by Whose direction the redemption of Israel from captivity is accomplished], and all the ends of the earth shall witness the salvation of our God.

Habakkuk 3:18 (AMPLIFIED) Yet I will rejoice in the Lord; I will exult in the {victorious} God of My Salvation!

Romans 1:16 (AMPLIFIED) For I am not ashamed of the Gospel (good news) of Christ, for it is God's power working unto Salvation [for deliverance from eternal death] to everyone who believes with a personal trust and a confident surrender and firm reliance, to the Jew first and also to the Greek.

2 Corinthians 6:2 (KJV) (For He saith, I have heard thee in a time accepted, and in the day of Salvation have I succored thee: behold now is the accepted time; behold, now is the day of Salvation.)

Philippians 2:12-14 (KJV) Wherefore, my beloved, as ye have always obeyed, not as in my presence only, but now much more in my absence, work out your own Salvation with fear and trembling. For it is God which worketh in you both to will and to do of His good pleasure. Do all things without murmurings and disputings.

Titus 2:11 (AMPLIFIED) For the grace of God (His unmerited favor and blessing) has come forward (appeared) for the deliverance from sin and the eternal Salvation for all mankind.

Hebrews 2:3 (KJV) How shall we escape, if we neglect so great Salvation; which at the first began to be spoken by the Lord, and was confirmed unto us by them that heard Him.

SUMMARY

Jesus is your Salvation and in Him is everything you need or will ever need. He redeemed you from a lost and dying world. If you have accepted your redemption that He took for you at the cross and realize that this life is temporal, but your eternity is forever, and it is up to you where you will spend it, it is either Heaven or hell there is no in between. You have a Heaven to gain and a hell to shun. Live for Jesus and you will have all the fun.

There is no fun or partying in hell as some people think. It is a place of torment in eternal fire forever. Heaven is beautiful more then words can describe and you will be with the Father and the Son and the Holy Ghost and all the Saints rejoicing with the Lord and loving Him and serving Him forever. He will give you the desires of your heart right now. Accept Him today in your heart, it is the best thing you will ever do in this life and the next, If you haven't already done so. Bless you always. Amen and Amen.

JOY

THE JOY OF THE LORD IS YOUR STRENGTH, HE HAS ALREADY GIVEN YOU HIS JOY TO LAUGH AT THE DEVIL, FOR THE DEVIL IS A LIAR.

Psalms 51:12 (KJV) Restore unto me the Joy of thy salvation; and uphold me with thy free spirit.

Psalms 126:5-6 (AMPLIFIED) They who sow in tears shall reap in Joy and Singing.

Isaiah 61:3 (AMPLIFIED) To grant [consolation and Joy] to those who mourn in Zion—to give them an ornament (a garland or diadem) of beauty instead of ashes, the oil of Joy instead of mourning, the garment (expressive) of praise instead of a heavy, burdened, and failing spirit that they may be called oaks of righteousness [lofty, strong, and magnificent, distinguished for uprightness, justice, and right standing with God], the planting of the Lord, that He may be glorified.

John 16:24 (AMPLIFIED) Up to this time you have not asked a [single] thing in My Name [as presenting all that I AM]; but now ask and keep on asking and you will receive, so that your Joy (gladness, delight) may be full and complete.

Romans 15:13 (AMPLIFIED) May the God of your hope so fill you with all Joy and Peace in believing [through the experience of your faith] that by the power of the Holy spirit you may abound and be overflowing (bubbling over) with hope.

Hebrews 12:2 (KJV) Looking unto Jesus the author and finisher of our faith: who for the Joy that was set before Him endured the cross, despising the shame, and is set down at the right hand or the throne of God.

James 1:2-4 (KJV) My brethren, count it all Joy when ye fall into divers temptations: Knowing this, that the trying of your faith worketh patience. But let patience have her perfect work, that ye may perfect and wanting nothing.

Peter 4:13 (KJV) But rejoice, in as much as ye are partakers of Christ's sufferings: that, when His glory shall be revealed, ye may be glad also with exceeding Joy.

SUMMARY

Jesus came to fill you with His Joy. He rejoices over you with dancing and singing. That is why He said to make merry in your heart by singing to each other with psalms and spiritual hymns. You can uplift one another and then His Joy will start to fill you, and the problems of this world will grow slowly dim in the light of His Glory and Grace.

Make a Joyful noise! The Lord says sing a song unto the Lord of His Goodness and His Mercy and of His Faithfulness and Love. Worship the Lord and Praise His Holy Name. Rejoice and again I say Rejoice. Amen and Amen.

FESTIVE REJOICING

REJOICE, REJOICE, FOR THIS IS THE DAY THE LORD HATH MADE SO REJOICE, AND BE GLAD IN IT, REJOICE IN THE PRESENCE OF THE KING OF YOUR LIFE.

Zephaniah 3:17 (AMPLIFIED) The Lord your God is in the midst of you, a Mighty One, a Savior [Who saves]! He will Rejoice over you with joy; He will rest [in silent satisfaction] and in His love He will be silent and make no mention [of past sins, or even recall them]: He will exult over you with singing.

Romans 5:2 (AMPLIFIED) Through Him also we have [our] access (entrance, introduction) by faith into this grace (state of God's favor) in which we [firmly and safely] stand. And let us Rejoice and exult in our hope of experiencing and enjoying the Glory of God.

Philippians 4:4 (AMPLIFIED) Rejoice in the Lord always [delight, gladden yourselves in Him]; again I say, Rejoice!

Psalms 37:4 (KJV) Delight thyself also in the Lord; and He shall give thee the desires of thine heart.

I Peter 1:8 (KJV) Whom having not seen, ye love; in whom, though now ye see Him not, yet believing, ye Rejoice with Joy unspeakable and full of Glory.

SUMMARY

Rejoice over the Lord the way He rejoices over you. He is so excited about you, that He is full of Joy just thinking about you and how much He loves you. His unconditional love is the way you should rejoice over your children and family and other people showing them how much you love them and are happy about them.

Rejoicing over them, letting them know they are special and precious to you and to Jesus. That is Festive Rejoicing when you make a concentrated effort to make another person know how much they mean to you and to Jesus. Blessings, Blessings! Amen and Amen.

GLORY

THE GLORY OF FATHER GOD, IS ALL THAT HE HAS, ALL THAT HE IS, SO YOU CAN CRY ABBA FATHER AND HE WILL REVEAL HIS GLORY WHICH IS HIMSELF TO YOU.

Psalms 19:1 (KJV) THE HEAVENS declare the Glory of God; and the firmament showeth His handiwork.

Psalms 104:31 (KJV) The Glory of the Lord shall endure for ever: the Lord shall rejoice in His works.

Isaiah 6:3 (KJV) And one cried unto another, and said. Holy, Holy, Holy, is the Lord of hosts: the whole earth is full of His Glory.

Isaiah 40:5 (KJV) And the Glory of the Lord shall be revealed, and all flesh shall sec it together: for the mouth of the Lord hath spoken it.

Isaiah 60:1 (AMPLIFIED) ARISE [from the depression and prostration in which circumstances have kept you—rise to a new life]! Shine (be radiant with the Glory of the Lord), for your light has come, and the Glory of the Lord has risen upon you!

Matthew 25:31 (KJV) When the Son of man shall come in His Glory, and all the holy angels with Him, then shall He sit upon the throne of His Glory.

John 1:14 (KJV) And the Word was made flesh, and dwelt among us, (and we beheld His Glory, the Glory as of the only begotten of the Father,) full of grace and truth.

John 1:14 (AMPLIFIED) And the Word (Christ) became flesh (human, incarnate) and tabernacled (fixed in His tent of flesh, lived awhile) among us; and we [actually] saw His Glory (His honor, His majesty), such Glory as an only begotten son receives from His father, full of grace (favor, loving- kindness and truth.

Galatians 6:14 (KJV) But God forbid that I should Glory, save in the cross of our Lord Jesus Christ, by whom the world is crucified unto me, and I unto the world.

Corinthians 3:18 (AMPLIFIED) And all of us, as with unveiled face, [because we] continued to behold [in the Word of God] as in a mirror the Glory of the Lord, arc constantly being transfigured into His very own image in ever increasing splendor and from one degree of Glory to another; [for this comes] from the Lord [who is] the Spirit.

Ephesians 1:6 (KJV) To the praise of the Glory of His Grace, wherein He hath made us accepted in the Beloved.

Colossians 1:27 (KJV) To whom God would make known what is the riches of the Glory of this mystery among the Gentiles: which is Christ in you, the hope of Glory:

Hebrews 1:3 (KJV) Who being the brightness of His Glory, and the express image of His person, and upholding all things by the word of His power, when He had by Himself purged our sins, sat down on the right hand of the Majesty on high:

Revelation 4:11 (KJV) Thou art worthy, O Lord, to receive Glory and honor and power: for thou hast created all things, and for thy pleasure they arc and were created.

Revelation 5:12 (KJV) Saying with a loud voice. Worthy is the Lamb that was slain to receive power, and riches, and Wisdom, and Strength, and Honor, and Glory, and Blessing.

SUMMARY

Jesus is worthy of all Glory and Honor and Praise, because He is the Alpha and Omega (the beginning and the end), so when you pray ask Him to show you His Glory. To show Himself strong in any situation you are facing and He will show off.

Get in agreement with His Word and His Glory will come in and illuminate the dark areas in your life and bring light into them. Things will be made fresh and new once again, better then before, because the Lord likes to show His Glory and show Himself strong He is an Almighty God. He alone has the power for you to reach out and touch that power and the Holy Spirit will fill you afresh and restore all the broken pieces in your life like no one else can. He is the third person of the Godhead.

Reach out and touch the Power and Glory of Jesus today. Your life will never be the same. In His Precious Holy Name. Amen and Amen.

EPILOGUE FOR THE COLOR WHITE

The color White is a very pure and cleansing color if you look in the sky it is White and blue so the earth is constantly being cleansed by the word of God from all the impurities, just like a Bride when she wears White on her wedding day. It means she is to be a virgin for her husband and so is he the same, because it means purity that her body has never been touched by him or any other man.

Likewise, the Lord is coming back soon for His bride that is to be holy and pure that has been cleansed by the blood of Jesus, that is why He said, "I am coming for a glorious church without spot or wrinkle a victorious church". If you have Jesus you are now part of His bride. The Bride of Christ and He is the Bride Groom. When babies get dedicated to the Lord the parents usually put them in White because they are pure and innocence, before the Lord until the age of reason. The Lord is also coming back in White riding a White horse because He is the Holy Lamb of God. Blessings, Blessings! Amen and Amen.

THE SEVEN COLORS OF THE RAINBOW: ARE RED, ORANGE, YELLOW, GREEN, BLUE, INDIGO, and PURPLE.

Not all of the colors are in this First Book but you can understand and see the Covenant that God gave to the World.

GENESIS 9:9-13 "And I, Behold, I establish my Covenant with you, and with your seed after you; And with every living creature that is with you, of the fowl, of the cattle, and of every beast of the earth with you; from all that go out of the Ark, to every beast of the earth. And I will establish my Covenant with you; neither shall all flesh be cut off any more by the waters of a flood; neither shall there anymore be a flood to destroy the earth. And God said, This is the token of the Covenant which I make between me and you and every living creature that is with you, for perpetual generations: I do set my bow in the cloud, and it shall be for a token of a Covenant between me and the earth."

THERE ARE SEVEN COMPLETION PROMISES CONTAINED WITHIN THIS COVENANT GOD MADE IN COLORS OF THE RAINBOW

God promises Atonement, Caution (yet Protection), Joy/ Honor, Hope/ Prosperity, Grace/ The Holy Spirit, the Kingdom of Heaven (Indigo-mixture of Blue and Purple) and Power/Kingship!

May the Lord Bless You and Keep You and cause His Face to Shine upon You always and may His Goodness and Mercy follow you all the days of Your Life. May You dwell in the House of the Lord forever. May His Favor surround You as a Shield everywhere You go and everything You do, everything that You put Your Hands to shall Prosper, and everywhere that You put Your Feet to is Holy Ground. Possess it for His Glory. Blessings Abound in Your Life Now and Always.

Arise and Shine for the Glory of the Lord is Risen upon You. Bless You. Amen, and Amen. I believe that this book will and has changed your life and if you have not accepted the love Jesus gave you at the Cross at Calvary, I pray and believe you will do that today for now is the day and appointed time of Salvation don't put off or delay. The greatest sacrifice that anyone ever gave the greatest gift of all time in this life and the next. So I will give you scriptures on what the word, (which is Jesus in the flesh) has to say about the truth.

It doesn't matter what you have in this life, you are still walking around as a walking dead person if you have not accepted the love that every person is looking for to fill them, you are still empty inside, and only Jesus can fill that. You will never be the same and you can be sure of your eternal destiny which can be Heaven. The choice is up to you, God gave you the right choice, His only-begotten Son.

Your Lord and Savior Jesus of Nazareth. A lot of people still believe He was a prophet well He was but He was also a Jewish Rabbi, and He also walked in all of the five-fold ministries, but the most important truth, He was and is the Son of the Living God. So look up for your redemption draweth nigh. Bless you Jesus loves you and so do I.

Also you can see why Noah's Ark was painted in Red, Blue and I believe Purple. The Covering of the Blood was on them to preserve them, which in that time they sacrificed lambs, for their sins. They were God's Royalty, Noah and his family were the only righteous at that time,(because he believed in God) so He revealed His will to Noah, that the whole earth would be destroyed by water, (which in that time they had never even seen rain). They all mocked Noah, but God preserved him and his family. Through that great flood, when it rained for forty days and forty nights, the same amount of time, that Jesus was tempted by the devil in the wilderness. Just like He wants to preserve you and your family, if you obey His voice (which is His Word).

Remember that all the races started again form Noah's three sons. God loved Noah because he was obedient, it also took him a hundred years to build the ark and they were all mocking him and laughing at him. Just like when God could tell you to do something for Him and step out in faith a lot of people could be laughing at you too. But do the will of God and the rewards are out of this world.

BROWN

MAN, EARTH.

Scriptures where it pertains to the color Brown in the Bible:

Genesis 1:10 (KJV) And God called the dry land Earth, and the gathering together of the waters called the Seas: and God saw that it was good.

Genesis 1:27 (KJV) So God created Man in His image, in the image of God created He him; male and female create He them.

Scriptures that pertain to the color Brown when you wear it :

MAN (OR WOMAN) ARE MADE IN THE IMAGE AND LIKENESS OF GOD.

Psalms 25:12-14 (AMPLIFIED) Who is the man (or woman) who reverently fears and worships the Lord? Him (or Her) shall He teach in the way that he(or she) should choose. He himself (or herself) shall dwell at ease, and his (or her) offspring shall inherit the land. The secret (of the sweet, satisfying companionship) of the Lord have they who fear (revere and worship) Him. And He will show them His covenant and reveal to them its {deep inner] meaning.

Ecclesiastics 7:29 (AMPLIFIED) Behold, this is the only [reason for it that] I have found; God made man (or woman) upright, but they [men and women] have sought out many devices [for evil].

Matthew 4:4 (AMPLIFIED) But He replied, It has been written, Man (or Woman) shall not live and be upheld and sustained by bread alone, but by every word that comes forth from the mouth of God.

2 Corinthians 4:16-18 (KJV) For which cause we faint not; but though our outward man (or woman) perish, yet the inward man (or woman) renewed day by day. For our light affliction, which is but for a moment, worketh for us a far more exceeding and eternal weight of glory. While we look not to at the things seen, but at the things which are not seen: for the things which are seen are temporal but the things which are not seen are eternal.

SUMMARY

Man (or Woman) was created in the Lord's image and after His likeness. He wanted someone to fellowship with, to talk to Him, Praise Him and Worship Him. That is the only reason you were created. Then He gave you this beautiful universe to enjoy because He loves you so much. There isn't anything that He won't do for you that is right and pleasing in His sight. Talk to the Lord today from your heart.

He knows what you are feeling before you say it. He wants you to talk to Him and fellowship with Him after all there isn't anybody like Him or that can compare to Him. He is the maker of this universe and created you to enjoy it. He is truly an awesome God. He cares for you and how you hurt or the tears you shed, because He hurts with you and wants only the best for you always. Be Blessed. Amen, and Amen.

EARTH

GOD CREATED THE HEAVENS AND THE EARTH, AND ALL THAT IS THEREIN.

Chronicles 16:31 (KJV) Let the heavens be glad, and let the earth rejoice: and let men (or women) say among the nations. The lord reigneth.

Psalms 24:1 (KJV) The Earth is the Lord's and the fullness thereof; the world, and they that dwell therein.

Psalms 33:5 (KJV) He loveth righteousness and judgment: the earth is full of the goodness of the Lord.

Psalms 72:19 (KJV) And Blessed be His glorious name for ever: and let the whole earth be filled with His glory; Amen, and Amen.

Psalms 89:11 (KJV) The heavens are thine, the earth also is thine: as for the world and the fullness thereof thou hast founded them.

Psalms 104:24 (KJV) O Lord, how manifold are thy works! in wisdom hast thou made them all: the earth is full of thy riches.

Ecclesiastes 1:4 (KJV) One generation passeth away, and another generation cometh: but the earth abideth for ever.

Isaiah 6:3 (KJV) And one cried unto another, and said, I Holy. Holy, Holy, is the Lord of hosts; the whole earth is full of His Glory.

Ezekiel 43:2 (KJV) And, Behold, the glory of the God of Israel came from the way of the east: and His voice was like a noise of many waters: and the earth shined with His glory.

SUMMARY

You can see that Father God spoke through Jesus and the Holy Spirit moved upon the face of the earth. The Lord created this earth with His words. You also are creating your world everyday with your words. There is creative power in your mouth, to speak blessing or cursing over your children, your family and your life so the miracle of this world did not come into being with a big bang, which is the evolution theory. Which is man's way of thinking, but only be the power of the spoken words of God.

There has been nothing that was created or ever will be created that was not from the King of Kings and Lord of Lords. Your miracle is in your mouth to frame your world, just like the Lord framed this world with His words.

Blessings of faith filled words in your life now and always. Amen, and Amen.

EPILOGUE FOR THE COLOR BROWN:

As you can see the color Brown is really an earth color and it represents, I believe, the earth after Adam and Eve fell. Just like in the fall of the year the leaves turn a few different colors but then they turn Brown and loose all the leaves till the spring.

They lie dormant for the winter and then in the spring new life comes into them and they begin to really live again. Well I believe that when Adam and Eve fell man took on the Adamic nature of that fall, and was left spiritually dead except for a few righteous men and women, when Jesus died He revived the world.

The world became spiritually alive again and everything was restored. If you receive that truth it is yours and you too can become spiritually alive again unto God. That is why you were born into this world with a sinful nature but Jesus has redeemed you as if you never sinned. God is so good and He is good all the time. Jesus has taken back the earth from Satan.

When Adam sinned and disobeyed God, satan was God of this world but Jesus redeemed the creation of Man (or Woman) in their fallen state and made them brand new again. Receive that great blessing today. Amen and Amen.

7

BLACK

DEATH TO SELF, HIDING PLACE, SIN, SHADOW OF HIS WINGS, AFFLICTION, DEATH, MOURNING, HUMILIATION, FAMINE, DISTRESS, SUFFERING, DARKNESS, EVIL, RECONCILING MEDIATOR, HUMILITY, EVIL OMENS, CURSES,

.*Scriptures where the color Black is mentioned in the Bible:*

Lamentations 4:8 (AMPLIFIED) [Prolonged famine has made] them Blacker than soot and darkness, they are not recognized in the streets. Their skin clings to their homes; it is withered and it has become [dry] like a stick.

Jeremiah 8:21 (KJV) For the hurt of the daughter of my people am I (Jeremiah) hurt; I am Black (in mourning) astonishment hath taken hold on me.

Jeremiah 14:2 (AMPLIFIED) Judah mourns and her gates languish; [her people] sit in Black [mourning garb] upon the ground, and the cry of Jerusalem goes up.

Revelation 6:5 (KJV) And when he had opened the third seal, I heard the third beast say, Come and see. And I beheld, and lo a Black horse; and he that sat on him had a pair of balances in his hand.

Scriptures that pertain to wearing the color Black:

DEATH TO SELF

RELATES TO THE DEATH AND RESURRECTION OF JESUS THAT SAYS WHEN YOU BECOME BORN AGAIN, YOUR OLD SIN NATURE IS GONE. WHEN HE DIED, YOU DIED WITH HIM, AND WHEN HE ROSE, YOU ROSE WITH HIM.

Corinthians 5:17 (AMPLIFIED) Therefore if any person is [engrafted] in Christ (the Messiah) he (or she) is a new creation (a new creature altogether); the old [previous moral and spiritual condition] has passed away. Behold, the fresh and new has come!

Ephesians 5:11 (AMPLIFIED) Take no part in and have no fellowship with the fruitless deeds and enterprises of darkness, but instead [let your lives be so in contrast as to] expose and reprove and convict them.

Romans 8:4-6 (AMPLIFIED) So that the righteous and just requirement of the Law might be fully met in us who live and move, not in the ways of the flesh but in the ways of the Spirit [our lives governed not by the standards and according to the dictates of the flesh, but controlled by the Holy Spirit].

For those who are according to the flesh and are controlled by its unholy desires set their minds on and pursue those things which gratify the flesh, but those who are according to the Spirit and are controlled by the desires of the Spirit set their minds on and seek those things which gratify the [Holy] Spirit. Now the mind of the flesh [which is sense and reason without the Holy Spirit] is death [death that comprises all the miseries arising from sin, both here and hereafter], but on the mind of the [Holy] Spirit is life and [soul] peace [both now and forever].

SUMMARY

So you can see one of the meanings of Black is death to your old self, which is the carnal nature and ways of the flesh. You are to walk in the Spirit so you don't fulfill the lusts of the flesh. The Lord wants you to know Him and what He suffered on that Cross. It is a reminder of the price He paid for you and for me. We will never know the cost of seeing our sins upon that Cross. He paid a debt that you could not pay, a debt that He did not owe. He went through the pain and the shame and the humiliation for the joy that was set before Him, that many would come to know the Truth, for He is the Truth and the Word which is real. The supernatural world is more real than this physical world. Whenever you pray and whatever you pray hast to be birthed in the supernatural before it manifests in the physical realm. If it isn't written, it isn't real. If you walk in the spirit of God, it can be done. Jesus did it and He said so can you. Be filled with the Holy Spirit and you will not fulfill the lusts of flesh.

HIDING PLACE

JESUS IS YOUR SHELTER FROM THE STORM, AND HE HIDES YOU FROM THE DARKNESS OF THE NIGHT IN YOUR LIFE.

Psalms 32:7 (KJV) Thou art my Hiding Place; thou shalt preserve me from trouble. Thou shalt compass me about with songs of deliverance. Selah.

Psalms 51:9 (AMPLIFIED) Hide your face from my sins and blot out all my guilt and inequities.

Psalms 119:11 (KJV) Thy word have I Hide in mine heart that I might not sin against thee.

Psalms 139:12 (KJV) Yes, the darkness Hideth not from thee; but the night shineth as the day: the darkness and the light are both alike to thee.

Corinthians 4:5 (AMPLIFIED) So do not make any hasty or premature judgments before the time when the Lord comes [again]; for He will both bring to light the secret things that are [now Hidden] in darkness and disclose and expose the [secret] aims (motives and purposes) of hearts. Then every man (or woman) will receive his (or her) (due) commendations from God.

Corinthians 4:3 (AMPLIFIED) But even if our Gospel (the glad tiding) also be Hidden (obscured and covered up with a veil that hinders the knowledge of God), it is Hidden [only] to those who are perishing and obscured [only] to those who are spiritually dying and veiled [only] to those who are lost.

Colossians 3:3 (AMPLIFIED) For [as far as this world is concerned] you have died, and your [new, real] life is Hidden with Christ in God.

SUMMARY

Jesus is your Hiding Place. He will hide you from your enemies and sudden destruction, and when He comes again He will bring to light all the darkness in this world, and expose it because He is the light in the darkness. He will bring those dark areas in your life to naught if you let Him. For where there is light, darkness cannot stay. A little bit of light lightens a room and where you couldn't see before you can now see clearly in that room. That can be compared with what happens in your heart. Jesus exposes the hidden intents of the heart.

And even in this world, they are really hiding themselves from the Glorious Light because, satan blinds the minds of men and women so they can't see the Truth unless they turn from their wicked ways and be saved, healed, delivered, free from worldly contamination, and be pure and holy in Jesus' sight. Run to Jesus today and let him be your hiding place and not the darkness of this world. Bless you. Amen and Amen.

SIN

ALL HAVE SINNED AND FELL SHORT OF THE GLORY OF GOD, THAT IS WHY SIN SEPARATES YOU FROM GOD AND YOU NEEDED A LORD AND SAVIOR.

Psalms 32:1 (AMPLIFIED) Blessed (Happy), fortunate to be envied) is he (or her) who has forgiveness of his transgression continually exercised upon him (or her), whose Sin is covered.

Isaiah 30:1 (KJV) Woe to the rebellious children, saith the Lord, that take counsel; but not of me: and that cover with a covering, but not of my spirit, that they may add Sin to Sin.

Romans 6:14 (KJV) For Sin shall not have dominion over you: for ye are not under the law, but under grace.

John 1:29 (AMPLIFIED) The next day John saw Jesus coming to him and said, Look! There is the Lamb of God, who takes away the sins of the world!

Romans 5:21 (KJV) For He hat h made Him to be Sin for us, who knew no Sin; that we might be made the righteousness of God in Him.

Ephesians 4:26 (AMPLIFIED) When angry, do not Sin; do not ever let your wrath (your exasperation, your fury or indignation) last until the sun goes down.

John 1:8-10 (AMPLIFIED) If we say we have no sin (refusing to admit that we are Sinners), we delude and lead ourselves astray, and the Truth [which the Gospel presents] is not in us [does not dwell in our hearts]. If we [freely] admit that we have Sinned and confess our Sins, He is faithful and just (true to His won nature and promises) and will forgive our Sins [dismiss our lawlessness] and [continuously] cleanse us from all unrighteousness [everything not in conformity to His will in purpose, thought, and action].

SUMMARY

If we say (claim) we have not Sinned, we contradict His Word and make Him out to be false and a liar, and His Word is not in us (the divine message of the Gospel is not in our hearts). Jesus took all your Sin at Calvary. He wiped them away so the only Sin anybody is guilty of is not accepting the great love that He poured out for you; not receiving the good news of His Gospel that He loved you so much to go through all the shame and the unbearable pain to His physical body to set you and the whole world free. Everyone has to believe and receive it. Everyone is looking for that kind of love. Jesus is the only one who can fill that emptiness inside of a man (or woman). Jesus paid a debt that you could never pay. Thank Him and praise Him for that great debt cancellation. Bless His Holy Name now and forevermore. Amen, and Amen.

SHADOW OF HIS WINGS

THE LORD WANTS TO PROTECT AND KEEP YOU UNDER HIS WINGS, TO PROTECT YOU FROM ALL EVIL, AND THE DARKNESS IN THIS WORLD SO STAY IN HIS LOVE.

Psalms 17:8 (KVJ) Keep me as the apple of thine eye, hide me under the Shadow of thy wings.

Psalm 91:1 (AMPLIFIED) He (or she) who dwells in the secret place of the Most High shall remain stable and fixed under the Shadow of the Almighty [Whose power no foe can withstand].

Psalm 57:1 (AMPLIFIED) Be merciful and gracious to me, O God, be merciful and gracious to me, for my soul takes refuge and finds shelter and confidence in You; yes, in the Shadow of Your Wings will I take refuge and be confident until calamities and destructive storms are passed.

SUMMARY

Jesus will keep you and protect you in the midst of trouble under the Shadow of His Wings. You will come through unharmed and shining in the Light of His Glory so that all who are around you will know it was Him that brought you through to dry land in the midst of the storm. And when you go through the fire you will not be burned because He will go through it with you. Rejoice, there is nothing to fear. Bless you. Amen, and Amen.

AFFLICTION

JESUS WAS AFFLICTED, BECAUSE HE IS THE WORD MADE FLESH SO WHEN YOU ARE BEING PERSECUTED FOR THE WORD OF GOD, JUST KNOW JESUS KNOWS WHAT YOU ARE GOING THROUGH AND HE WILL TAKE YOU THROUGH, TURN TO HIM.

Timothy 1:8-10 (KJV) Be not thou therefore ashamed of the testimony of our Lord, nor of me, his prisoner; but be thou partaker of the afflictions of the Gospel according to the power of God; Who hath saved us, and called us with a holy calling, not according to our works but according to his own purpose and grace, which was given us in Christ Jesus before the world began but is now made manifest by the appearing of our Savior Jesus Christ, who hath abolished death, and hath brought life and immortality to light through the Gospel.

James 1:27 (AMPLIFIED) External religious worship [religion as it is expressed in outward acts] that is pure and unblemished in the sight of God the Father is this: to visit and help and care for the orphans and widows in their affliction and need, and to keep oneself unspotted and uncontaminated from the world.

Psalms 140:12 (KJV) I know that the Lord will maintain the cause of the Afflicted, and the right of the poor.

Proverbs 15:15 (AMPLIFIED) All the days of the desponding and Afflicted are made evil [by anxious thought and forebodings], but he (or she) who has a heart has a continual feast [regardless of circumstances].

Psalms 25:18 (AMPLIFIED) Behold my Affliction and my pain and forgive all my sins [of thinking and doing].

Psalms 34:17-20 (KJV) The righteous cry, and the Lord heareth, and delivereth them out of all their troubles. The Lord is nigh unto them that are of a broken heart; and saveth such as be of a contrite spirit. Many are the Afflictions of the righteous: but the Lord delivereth him (or her) out of them all. He keepeth all his (or her) bones; not one of them is broken.

SUMMARY

The Lord will keep you in your afflictions and will deliver you out of them all. Don't quit and don't give up. Remain in His presence and keep your eyes on Jesus. Listen to the sweet, precious Holy Spirit who leads and guides you into all the ways you should go. He will lead you down the right path with Jesus. You will not fail because He did not fail. You can make it if you are persistent. Persistence builds character and strength. You can't do it on your own strength or in the flesh. Jesus said not by might, not by power, but by my spirit saith the Lord. Be bold, and be strong, for the Lord thy God is with thee.

Say I am not afraid; I am not dismayed for I keep walking in faith and victory, for the Lord they God is with me always, and He can see and will not fail me. Blessings, Blessings! Amen, and Amen.

DEATH

YOU WILL LIVE FOREVER, EITHER IN HEAVEN OR IN HELL, THERE IS NO IN BETWEEN, SO CHOOSE LIFE THAT YOU AND YOUR SEED MAY LIVE FOREVER IN THE PRESENCE OF GOD.

Psalms 68:20 (AMPLIFIED) God is to us a God of deliverances and salvation; and to God, The Lord, belongs escape from Death [setting us free].

Isaiah 25:8 (AMPLIFIED) He will swallow up death [in victory; He will abolish Death forever]. And the Lord God will wipe away tears from all faces; and the reproach of His people He will take away from all the earth; for the Lord has spoken it.

St. Matthew 16:28 (KJV) Verify I say unto you, there be some standing here which shall not taste of death, 'til they see the son of man coming in His kingdom.

St. John 5:24 (AMPLIFIED) I assure you, most solemnly I tell you, the person whose ears are open to My words [who listens to My message] and believes and trusts in and clings to and relies on Him Who sent Me has (now possesses eternal life. And he (or she) does not come into judgment [does not incur sentence of judgment, will not come under condemnation], but he (or she) has already passed over out of death into life.

Romans 8:2 (KJV) For the law of the Spirit of life in Christ Jesus hath made me free from the law of sin and Death.

Corinthians 15:55 (KJV) O Death, where is thy sting? O grave where is they victory?

Philippians 2:8 (AMPLIFIED) And after He had appeared in human form, He abased and humbled Himself [still further] and carried His obedience to the extreme Death, even the Death of the Cross!

Hebrews 2:9 (AMPLIFIED) But we are able to see Jesus, who was ranked lower than the angels for a little while, crowned with glory and honor because of His having suffered Death, in order that by the grace (unmerited favor) of God [to us sinners] He might experience Death for every individual person.

Revelation 21:4 (KJV) And God shall wipe away all tears from their eyes, and there shall be no more Death, neither sorrow, nor crying, neither shall there be any more pain, for the former things are passed away.

SUMMARY

There really is no death for the believer; you just shed your earth suit but you will go from life to life and be forever with the Lord. Jesus is coming very soon, sooner than believers imagine, because we are often distracted with earthly things not seeing in the spiritual what is really going on. So prepare and look up, for your redemption draweth nigh. The Lord said them that remain will be caught in a twinkling of an eye, meaning the ones that would be here for His second coming would not taste physical Death. So, rejoice for Jesus is coming soon. Amen

MOURNING

JESUS WILL TURN YOUR MOURNNG INTO LAUGHTER AND JOY.

Psalms 5:4 (AMPLIFIED) Blessed and enviably happy [with a happiness produced by the experience of God's favor and especially conditioned by the revelation of His matchless grace] are those who mourn, for they shall be comforted!

Psalms 30:11 (KJV) Thou hast turned for me my Mourning into dancing; thou hast put off my sackcloth, and girded me with gladness; To the end that my glory may sing praise to Thee and not be silent, O Lord my God, I will give thanks unto Thee forever.

Isaiah 61:3 (KJV) To appoint into them that Mourn in Zion, to give unto them beauty for ashes, the oil of joy for Mourning, the garment of praise for the spirit of heaviness; that they might be called trees of righteousness, the planting of the Lord, that He might be glorified.

Jeremiah 31:13 (AMPLIFIED) Then will the maidens rejoice in the dance, and the young men and old together. For I will turn their Mourning into joy and will comfort them and make them rejoice after their sorrow.

SUMMARY

Jesus sees all of your tears and fears, and He said weeping may endure for the night but joy comes in the morning. Sometimes when the pressures of this life can become so overwhelming you can sometimes can feel all alone and say to yourself Lord, where are you and how could this have happened in my life? But you are never alone, look at Joseph's life when he was thrown into the pit, sold as a slave and then falsely accused, sent to prison for a crime he didn't commit.

Then after God gave him the gift of knowing what dreams meant, then he was brought to the Pharaoh and asked to give him the meaning of his dreams and when he did, he was almost head of all Egypt.(which at that time ruled the world).. I am sure he cried out to the Lord My God, My God why hast thou forsaken me, when he went through all those afflictions, but he was faithful to God and God raised him up to the most powerful position in all the world. That is why the Lord says to seek after His divine wisdom and not the world's wisdom, which is devilish.

Through St. Paul, Jesus also said, learn how to abased and abound in every situation, knowing that even when you may feel alone, the Lord said I will never leave you or forsake you in time of trouble. Call on me and I will answer you. If you don't stop and keep pressing in for the prize, He will turn your mourning into dancing for all those around you to see that He is God and there is no other. Bless you abundantly. Amen!!!

HUMILIATION

JESUS SUFFERED THE GREATEST HUMILATION, AT THE CORSS. HE WAS LAUGHED AT AND SCOFFED AT AND MOCKED, HE ALSO WAS DESPISED AND REJECTED OF MEN AND WOMEN, AND THEY SAID TO HIM WHILE HE WAS DYING FOR YOU AND FOR ME [HAIL KING OF THE JEWS.

Matthew 23:12 (AMPLIFIED) Whoever exalts himself (or herself) [with haughtiness and empty pride] shall be humbled (brought low), and whoever humbles himself (or herself) [whoever has a modest opinion of himself (or herself) and behaves accordingly] shall be raised to honor.

Hebrews 12:2 (AMPLIFIED) Looking away [from all that will distract] to Jesus, Who is the Leader and the Source of our faith [giving the first incentive for our belief] and is also its Finisher [bringing it to maturity and perfection]. He, for the joy [of obtaining the prize] that was set before Him, endured the cross, despising and ignoring the Shame and is now seated at the right hand of the throne of God.

SUMMARY

When you suffer humiliation, think of Jesus, the living Son of God who was willing to suffer what He did, and He was innocent. Sometimes you may do something that causes you to feel humiliated, and sometimes you may not do anything, but the devil may be trying to bring up past sins and mistakes.

Remember with Jesus you are not guilty. He paid the price for you. So run to Him and not from Him, and you will be compensated and justified. He will work it out for you. Blessings, Blessings! Amen, and Amen.

FAMINE

JESUS SAID THERE WOULD BE FAMINE AND FLOODS AND EARTHQUAKES IN THESE TIMES BUT, FEAR NOT, I AM WITH YOU ALWAYS, EVEN UNTIL THE END OF THE AGE.

Genesis 12:10 (KJV) And there was a Famine in the land; and Abraham went down into Egypt to sojourn there for the Famine was grievous in the land.

Job 5:20 (KJV) In Famine, He shall redeem thee from death; and in war, from the power of the sword.

Psalms 33:19 (KJV) To deliver their soul from death, and to keep them alive in Famine.

Amos 8:11 (AMPLIFIED) Behold, the days are coming, says the Lord God, when I will send a Famine in the land, not a Famine of bread, nor a thirst for water, but a [Famine] for hearing the words of the Lord.

SUMMARY

Jesus said there would be Famine and pestilence and drought in the land. The spiritual is always first; then it manifests itself in the physical world. The earth is in travail with groaning waiting for the coming of the Lord, as witnessed by the storms and tornados and floods and hurricanes that are happening all over the world. I know the Lord said these things must come to pass, which would be the beginning of sorrows.

People are in fear because their hearts are in famine. Not knowing what to do or what is about to happen next. They have hardened their hearts to the truth the incorruptible and unchanging word of God.

The Lord's word is truth; not doing things our way but His way. He said you will always have the poor with you but when you give to the poor you lend to the Lord and He will repay you.

Remember, if God has to send a bird to feed you He will do it. He will make water flow from the rocks if He has to. The word says if you don't praise Him, the rocks will cry out and I don't want the rocks to cry out. Praise Him in your time of need and remember the praises go up, the blessings come down, like showers of a downpour of rain Praise the Lord for He is worthy from the rising of the sun to the going down of the same.

DISTRESS

JESUS SAID THE RIGHTEOUS CRY AND I THE LORD HEAR, AND

DELIVER THEM OUT OF ALL THEIR TROUBLES.

Genesis 35:3 (KJV) And let us arise, and go up to Bethel; and I (Jacob) will make there an altar unto God, who answered me in the day of my Distress, and was with me in the way which I went.

Psalms 4:1 (AMPLIFIED) Answer me when I call, O God of my righteousness (uprightness, justice and right standing with You)! You have freed me when I was hemmed in and enlarged me when I was in Distress; have mercy upon me and hear my prayer.

Psalms 120:1 (AMPLIFIED) In my Distress I cried to the Lord, and He answered me.

Zephaniah 1:14-15 (KJV) The great day of the Lord is near, it is near, and hasteth greatly, even the voice of the day of the Lord: the mighty man (or woman) shall cry there bitterly. That day is a day of wrath, a day of trouble and Distress, a day of wasteness and desolation, a day of darkness and gloominess, a day of clouds and thick darkness.

St. Luke 21:25 (KJV) And there shall be signs in the sun, and in the moon, and in the stars, and upon the earth Distress of nations, with perplexity; the sea and the waves roaring.

Romans 8:35 (KJV) Who shall separate us from the love of Christ? Shall tribulation, or Distress, or persecution, or famine, or nakedness, or peril, or sword?

SUMMARY

Jesus said these you are now living in Distressful times but He is there to keep you strong in His strength and to let the Sweet Precious Holy Spirit to lead and guide you into His divine wisdom.

He will direct you in every situation to avoid calamities and destructions that are around and about you. You have to be sensitive to His voice so that you listen to the voice of the Good Shepherd, and the voice of the stranger, you will not follow.

It is more important in these times to be right with the Holy Spirit because He is your best friend and He will protect you from all Distresses, if you are listening to that still small voice. Blessings, Blessings Amen and Amen!!!

SUFFERING

JESUS SUFFERED FOR YOU AND HE WAS PERSECUTED FOR THE TRUTH, AND HE SAID THAT YOU NEED TO DIE DAILY IN HIS SUFFERING, THAT YOU WILL BE PERSECUTED FOR THE WORD WHICH IS JESUS BUT COUNT IT ALL JOY.

Psalms 55:22 (KJV) Cast they burden upon the Lord, and He shall sustain thee: He shall never Suffer the righteous to be moved.

Psalms 121:3 (KJV) He will not Suffer they foot to be moved: He that keepeth thee will not slumber.

Romans 8:18 (KJV) For I reckon that the Sufferings of this present time are not worthy to be compared with the glory which shall be revealed in us.

Hebrews 2:10 (AMPLIFIED) For it was an act worthy [of God] and fitting [to the divine nature] that He, for Whose sake by Whom all things have their existence, in bringing many sons into glory, should make the Pioneer of their salvation perfect [should bring to maturity the human experience necessary to be perfectly equipped for His office as High Priest] through Suffering.

Hebrews 2:18 (AMPLIFIED) For because He Himself [in His humanity] has Suffered in being tempted (tested and tried). He is able [immediately] to run to the cry of (assist, relieve) those who are being tempted and tested and tried [and who therefore are being exposed to Suffering].

SUMMARY

Jesus and the disciples Suffered so you are not above your Master. Jesus will come to you and comfort you in the midst of the Suffering. Jesus wants to live inside of you so that everyone around you can see and know it was Him, who strengthened you, wrapped His arms around you. Jesus said you can make it, you can do it, as if you were healed from a disease and you are now walking in divine health, or going through a financial crisis and you are now debt free, when the rest of the world is in a financial slump.

It is really an honor to see how much the Lord loves you and how much He cares when it seems that no one else does. These are His blessings beyond measure for you and your family. Amen, and Amen.

DARKNESS

JESUS SAID FOR YOU TO BE THE LIGHT IN THE DARKNESS OF THIS WORLD, JUST LIKE HE CAME TO MANIFEST HIS LIGHT.

Genesis 1:2 (AMPLIFIED) The earth was without form and an empty waste, and Darkness was upon the face of the very great deep. The Spirit of God was moving (hovering, brooding) over the face of the waters.

Isaiah 5:20 (AMPLIFIED) Woe to those who call evil good and good evil, who put Darkness for light and light for Darkness, who put bitter for sweet and sweet for bitter!

Isaiah 9:2 (AMPLIFIED) The people who walked in Darkness have seen a great Light; those who dwelt in the land of intense Darkness and the shadow of death, upon them has the Light shined.

Matthew 4:16 (AMPLIFIED) The people who sat (dwelt, enveloped) in Darkness have seen a great Light, and for those who sat in the land and shadow of death, Light has dawned.

John 1:5 (AMPLIFIED) And the Light shines on in the Darkness. For the darkness has never overpowered it [put it out or absorbed it or appropriated it, and is unreceptive to it].

Romans 13:12 (KJV) The night is far spent, the day is at hand: let us therefore cast off the works of Darkness, and let us put on the armor of light.

Corinthians 4:6 (KJV) For God, who commanded the light to shine out of Darkness, "hath shined in our hearts, to give the light of the knowledge of the glory of God in the face of Jesus Christ."

John 1:5 (KJV) This then is the message which we have heard of Him, and declare unto you, that god is the light, and in Him is no Darkness at all.

SUMMARY

Jesus is the light of the world; he has overcome all of the Darkness in it. Let his light shine through you. Do not neglect so great an honor. You are already His vessel that He has made. His light is to be seen through you so that everyone around you can see the Jesus in you. It is no longer that you live, but Christ liveth in you. You are His chosen vessel of Honor, chosen through His grace and for His glory.

Many people are in the valley of decision. They will be drawn to you and may not know why. Let that light of the world, which is Jesus shine, shine and shine, show His love, be His example. With a smile on your face, go that extra mile for someone. Give them a hug. Let them see and feel Jesus. Bless you always. Amen, and Amen.

EVIL

JESUS CAME TO DESTROY THE WORKS OF DARKNESS, AND ALLTHE EVIL THAT EXISTS IN THE WORLD TODAY. THEREFORE HE MADE YOU MORE THAN A CONQUERER IN THIS LIFE.

Psalms 91:10 (KJV) There shall be no Evil befall thee, neither shall any plague come nigh thy dwelling.

Jeremiah 29:11 (AMPLIFIED) For I know the thoughts and plans that I have for you, says the Lord, thoughts and plans for welfare and peace and not for Evil. Go give you hope in your final outcome.

Amos 5:14 (AMPLIFIED) Seek (inquire for and require) good and not Evil that you may live, and so the Lord, the God of hosts, will be with you, as you have said.

St. Matthew 5:11-12 (AMPLIFIED) Blessed (happy, to be envied, and spiritually prosperous – with life-joy and satisfaction in God's favor and salvation, regardless of your outward condition) are you when people revile you and persecute you and say all kinds of Evil things against you falsely on My account. Be glad and supremely joyful, for your reward in heaven is great (strong and intense), for in this same way people persecuted the prophets who were before you.

Romans 12:21 (AMPLIFIED) Do not let yourself be overcome by Evil, but overcome (master) Evil with good.

Ephesians 5:15-16 (AMPLIFIED) Look carefully then how you walk! Live purposefully and worthily and accurately, not as the unwise and witless, but as wise (sensible, intelligent people). Making the very most of the time [buying up each opportunity], because the days are Evil.

John 1:11 (AMPLIFIED) Beloved, do not imitate Evil, but imitate good. He (or she) who does good is of God; he (or she) who does Evil has not seen (discerned or experienced) God [has enjoyed no vision of Him and does not know Him at all].

SUMMARY

Jesus always returned good for Evil and so should you. This is what the Bible means when the Lord tells you to turn the other cheek. It doesn't mean to let someone physically harm you but when someone is accusing you, unjustly, do not retaliate. When you don't answer them, whatever darts are being thrown at you turns back on them. Jesus said if your enemy is hungry, feed her. If she is naked, clothe her. Always return good for Evil. Vengeance is mine saith the Lord, and I will repay you. The Lord will repay you for the wrong that has been done to you. Walk in love and not in fear. Nothing and no one can harm you. Blessings of Mercy and Grace! Amen, and Amen.

RECONCILING MEDIATOR

JESUS IS YOUR RECONCILING MEDIATOR IN ALL THINGS, AND AT ALL TIMES HIS BLOOD HAS CLEANSED YOU WHITER THAN SNOW.

Corinthians 5:20-21 (AMPLIFIED) So we are Christ's ambassadors, God making His appeal, as it were, thought us. We [as Christ's personal representatives] beg you for His sake to lay hold of the divine favor [now offered you] and be Reconciled to God. For our sake He made Christ [virtually] to be sin Who knew no sin, so that in and through Him we might become [endued with, viewed as being in, and examples of] the righteousness of God [what we ought to be, approved and acceptable and in right relationship with Him, by His goodness].

Romans 5:10 (AMPLIFIED) For if while we were enemies we were Reconciled to God through the death of His Son, it is much more [certain], now that we are Reconciled, that we shall be saved (daily delivered from sin's dominion0 through His [resurrection] life.

SUMMARY

Jesus is the Reconciling Mediator between Father God and man (or woman). He constantly intercedes for you. When you accept Jesus as your Lord and Savior, you have already been Reconciled. If you have not been Reconciled but are reading this book, Jesus is reaching out to you saying, come unto me, you that are heavy laden and I will give you rest for your mind, will and emotions.

Fear not, for I will be with you, even unto the end of this age, I will walk with you and talk with you and be your friend. I will never turn away from you. You can call on me any time, day or night, and I will answer you. For my ways are higher than your ways, and my ways are certain. I will never fail you, for I love you with an everlasting love. Now and forever, Blessings, Blessings of the Holy Ghost's fire in your life. Amen!

HUMILITY

JESUS SHOWED HIS HUMILITY ON THE CROSS AND GAVE YOU THE EXAMPLE OF TRUE HUMILITY, FOR IF YOU HUMBLE YOURSELF YOU SHALL BE EXHALTED, BUT IF YOU EXHALT YOURSLEF YOU SHALL BE HUMBLED.

Proverbs 15:23 (AMPLIFIED) The reverent and worshipful fear of the Lord brings instruction in Wisdom, and Humility comes before Honor.

Proverbs 22:4 (KJV) By Humility and the fear of the Lord are Riches, and Honor, and Life.

Acts 20:19 (KJV) Serving the Lord with all Humility of mind, and with many tears, and temptations, this befell me by the lying in wait of the Jews.

1 Peter 5:5 (AMPLIFIED) Likewise, you who are younger and of lesser rank, be subject to the elders (the ministers and spiritual guides of the church) [giving them due respect and yielding to their counsel].

Clothe (apron) yourselves, all of you, with Humility [as the garb of a servant, so that its covering cannot possibly be stripped from you, with freedom from pride and arrogance] toward one another. For God sets Himself against the proud (the insolent, the overbearing, the disdainful, the presumptuous, the boastful) – [and He opposes, frustrates, and defeats them], but gives grace (favor, blessing) to the Humble.

SUMMARY

Jesus said, Humility comes before Honor. The spirit of man (or woman) should rule the flesh to overcome pride. Jesus was a humble servant. Like any good leader, Jesus always humbled Himself, even to His death on the cross. He knew He was the Son of the Living God.

In the Garden of Gethsemane when Peter cut off the high priest's ear, Jesus put his ear back in place and healed him. And He said to Peter, did you not know that I could call for ten thousand of legions of angels to just take Him off this earth? But He humbled himself by going to the Cross for you and for me. When we were still sinners, He was willing to lay His life down for you and me. Jesus was obedient to his death.

No greater sacrifice has ever been made or will ever be made. Jesus was the supreme sacrifice. Humble yourself under His mighty hand and He will raise you up in due season. Be blessed, and run to His outstretched arms of love today. Amen, and Amen.

EVIL OMENS

JESUS IS NOT THE AUTHOR OF EVIL, ALL EVIL COMES FROM THE EVIL ONE, THE DEVILI HAVE SEEN AND HEARD PEOPLE BLAME GOD FOR EVIL, INSTEASD OF REALIZING THERE IS A BAD DEVIL BUT THERE IS A GOOD GOD AND THERE IS NO EVIL AT ALL IN HIM.

Revelation 6:8 (AMPLIFIED) So I looked, and behold, an ashy pale horse (black and blue as if made so by bruising), and it's rider's name was Death, and Hades (the realm of the dead) followed him closely. And they were given authority and power over a fourth part of the earth to kill with the sword and with famine and with plague (pestilence, disease) and with wild beasts of the earth.

Revelation 12:9 (AMPLIFIED) And the huge dragon was cast down and out – that age old serpent, who is called the Devil and Satan, he who is the seducer (deceiver) of all humanity the world over, he was forced out and down to the earth, and his angels were flung out along with him.

Genesis 3:14 (AMPLIFIED) And the Lord God said to the serpent, Because you have done this, you are cursed above all (domestic) animals and above every [wild] living thing of the field, upon your belly you shall go, and you shall eat dust [and what it contains] all the days of your life.

Revelation 9:20-21 (AMPLIFIED) And the rest of humanity who were not killed by those plagues even then did not repent of [the worship of] the works of their [own] hands, so as to cease paying homage to the demons and idols of gold and silver and bronze and stone and wood, which can neither see nor hear nor move. And they did not repent of their murders or their practice of magic (sorceries) or their sexual vice or their thefts.

SUMMARY

Jesus does not have any part with evil. He came to give you a more abundant life. There were things done by Almighty God, to the children of disobedience in the Old Testament, but I believe they brought it upon themselves. God saw that man could not keep the law and He planted His most precious seed, Jesus.

Satan is the author of evil and worshipping false gods, which is giving honor to him. Only one time God will pour out His wrath upon this world and that is during the tribulation period. If you have Jesus in your heart and believe that Jesus is coming soon for His Bride, the church, His body of believers, then you will not be there for the terrible time on this earth. Blessings, Blessings! Amen, and Amen.

CURSES

JESUS SAID CHOOSE THIS DAY WHO YOU WILL SERVE, CHOOSE LIFE OR DEATH, BLESSING OR CURSING. THE CHOICE IS YOURS, THERFORE CHOOSE LIFE AND LIVE.

Genesis 8:21-22 (AMPLIFIED) When the Lord smelled the pleasing odor [a scent of satisfaction to His heart], the Lord said to Himself, I will never again curse the ground because of man (or woman), for the imagination (the strong desire) of man's (or woman's) heart is evil and wicked from his (or her) youth; neither will I ever again miss and destroy every living thing, as I have done. While the earth remains, seedtimes and harvest, cold and heat, summer and winter, and day and night shall not cease.

Deuteronomy 11:26-28 (KJV) Behold I set before you this day a blessing and a curse. A blessing, if ye obey the commandments of the Lord your God, which I command you this day: And a curse, if ye will not obey the commandments of the Lord your God; but turn aside out of the way which I command you this day, to go after other gods, which ye have not known.

Romans 12:14 (AMPLIFIED) Bless those who persecute you [who are cruel in their attitude toward you]; bless and do not curse them.

Galatians 3:13-14 (KJV) Chris hath redeemed us from the curse of the law, being made a curse for us, for it is written. Cursed is every one that hangeth or a tree, that the blessings of Abraham might come on the Gentiles through Jesus Christ, that we might receive the promise of the Spirit through faith.

SUMMARY

Jesus became a Curse for you when He hung on that Cross so that you can walk in the blessings of the New Abrahamic Covenant. Also nobody can put a Curse on you unless you receive it. The Word of God is clear that you are now blessed, with all spiritual blessings in heavenly places. It is God's will for you to walk in them.

Many curse themselves with their mouths and wonder why curses have come upon them. That is why the Lord says to choose life, choose to believe His word above all the evil negativity of the world, Know if it isn't written, it isn't real. Watch the words that you speak, let yours be words of life, not of death, and you will see the blessings of the Lord flowing into your life and family and ministry and health and finances. Amen, and Amen.

EPILOGUE FOR THE COLOR BLACK:

So you have seen by reading the Chapter on Black, why they use it in Satanic rituals and why they tend to wear it at funerals. Why some religions use it, because it does relate to mourning and affliction and guilt and shame, but it also pertains to the death of your old, sinful nature when you become Born Again.

Black is not really a color. It has no brightness. The Devil also uses black and red because he knows he is in darkness. He also knows the power of the color red. When people worship him they are giving a defeated foe power that he only has if you give it to him. The devil will give you the greed of this world, the violence this world has to offer, the drugs, the sexual perversion, and the angers and hate of men (and women) trying to get ahead.

For a time you may think you are getting ahead, then comes the destruction that he offers when he is done using you, and abusing you.

The devil has no mercy or compassion for you. He just wants to use you to get his evil purposes done. He wants to keep you always from the love of Jesus and put curses in your life. He is the great deceiver who sneaks in and then you will feel his sting, just like he did in the Garden to Eve. Remember, there is pleasure in sin for a season, then comes spiritual death. Be wise as a serpent but harmless as a dove and always walk in love. Give no place to Him, get into the world of God. It will bring light and love into your life. Blessings fall on you like showers of rain.

FINAL EPILOGUE FOR THE COLORS

This book will and has already changed your life forever, because of the Love that has been portrayed to you and the love that Jesus gave you on the Cross at Calvary. I pray and believe you will do that today. For now is the appointed time for your Salvation, don't put it off or delay the greatest sacrifice that anyone ever gave.

This is the greatest gift of all time in this life and the next. So I will give you the scriptures on what the Word, which is Jesus in the flesh, has to say about the Truth. It doesn't matter what you have done in this life, or what you have or don't have if you have not accepted the truth you are a spiritually dead person. If you have just known religion and not life, and still looking for the love that only Jesus can fill and not the traditions of men and women. Then let His love fill you to overflowing and you can be sure that Heaven is your Eternal destiny.

The choice is yours to make not your mother or your father's only you can make it for yourself. God already gave you the right choice. His only begotten Son Jesus Christ. He alone is Lord and Savior.

The same God (of Abraham, Isaac and Jacob) Jesus of Nazareth was a Jewish Rabbi and walked in the whole Five-Fold Ministry. This means Jesus was / is a Pastor, Preacher, Teacher, Prophet and a Apostle. But the most important truth is He is the Son of the Living God. Jesus is the name above all names.

Every knee shall bow to that name in Heaven and Earth and confess He is Lord. Amen and Amen (let it be so).

I believe this book has been a wonderful experience for you on the world of colors. and to be aware what colors mean around you and how you can change the whole atmosphere in your home. Also the colors you put on your body everyday, what they mean in connection with the Word of God. I believe this has given you more revelation in the things of God. How God created everything for a reason, even the stones have meaning. That is why He said if you don't praise Him even the rocks will cry out. For more information on my Ministry which is

NEW BEGINNINGS—- BEAUTY FOR ASHES ——-WOMEN'S MINISTRY YOU CAN WRITE ME AT:

DOMINIQUE R. DELLA FERA
BEAUTY FOR ASHES MINISTRY
8001 Maple Ave. Apt. 408
Pennsauken, N.J. 08109
Or e-mail me at dominiquedellafera@yahoo.com

Say this Prayer with all of your heart and confess with your mouth out loud that JESUS is LORD and your life will never be the same. You will be Heaven bound so that you will be sure of your salvation. The Word says call on the name of Jesus and you shall be saved, wearing your crown as you will be clothed in the Robe of Jesus Righteousness not your own (for His is much better). Hear Him say, I welcome you to the Kingdom of God, out of the darkness into My Glorious this Light.

PRAYER:

JESUS COME INTO MY HEART, I WANT TO LIVE FOR YOU AND I SURRENDER ALL OF MYSELF TO YOU. I ASK FORGIVENESS OF THE ONLY SIN FOR WHICH I AM GUILITY OF REJECTING YOU. I WILL NEVER REJECT YOU AGAIN. THANK YOU JESUS FOR SAVING ME AND HEALING ME AND DELIVERING ME. AMEN AND AMEN

AND NOW I ASK YOU FATHER GOD TO BAPTIZE ME WITH THE INFILLING OF THE HOLY SPIRIT, TO BE FILLED WITH YOUR SPIRIT, AND TO PRAY IN YOUR HEAVENLY LANGUAGE. I THANK

YOU FOR THESE THINGS IN JESUS NAME. AMEN AND AMEN

AND I THANK YOU LORD FOR SENDING INTO MY LIFE THE PERFECT ANOINTED LABORERS ACROSS MY PATH TO CONTINUE MY WALK WITH YOU AND TO LEAD AND GUIDE ME INTO ALL YOUR TRUTH.

AND NO WEAPON FORMED AGAINST ME SHALL PROSPER OR YOUR PERFECT PLAN AND PURPOSE IN MY LIFE. AND I DECLARE AND DEGREE THIS IN YOUR NAME AND IT SHALL BE ESTABLISHED. THANK YOU JESUS FOR SAVING ME HEALING ME AND DELIVERING ME RIGHT NOW. AMEN

www.ingramcontent.com/pod-product-compliance
Lightning Source LLC
Chambersburg PA
CBHW041116120626
46547CB00019B/2739

* 9 7 8 1 9 6 4 9 2 9 6 7 5 *